THE ADJUSTABLE AREA MAN-TO-MAN PRESS

BURRALL PAYE

Harding Press
Haworth, New Jersey 07641

ght © 1998 *by*

rding Press

Library of Congress Cataloging-in-Publication Data

Paye, Burrall, 1938-
    The adjustable area man-to-man press / Burrall Paye.
      p.   cm.
    ISBN 1-890450-00-6 (pbk.)
    1. Basketball--Defense. 2. Basketball--Coaching.   I. Title.
  GV888.P366   1997
  796.323'2--dc21   97-33181
                                                              CIP

ISBN 1-890450-00-6

Printed in the United States of America

HARDING PRESS
P.O. Box 141
Haworth, NJ 07641

Books by and for the coaching profession

To be a good teacher of the game of basketball a coach must surround himself with great assistants and better-than-average players. From my very first assistant, Delbert Marks, to my very last, Marshall Ashford, I've been blessed. In between there were Dave Bentley, Donnie Pruitt, Dickie Cornette (father of Miss America, Leanza Cornette), Lenny Mosser, Barry Hamler, and Andy Gray. Those coaches really knew how to teach this great game.

From that first team in 1960, Bill Justus, Buster Ramey, Leo Sage, Steve Dill, Nicky Howard, and Mike Easterly, to that last team in 1996, Richard Wilson, Brad Dunleavy, R. J. Reynolds, Charles Burnette, Sterling Tate, and James Stokes—and all the ones in between who are too numerous to name—I was overly blessed. Those players could really play this game.

Thanks for the wonderful ride.

Contents

What This Book Will Do for You

The adjustable area man-to-man press is just that: It is adjustable, it occurs in a predetermined area of the court, and it is man to man.

Because it is adjustable you can use it to take any player out of his game. It will completely stop the great dribbling point guard; it will eliminate a post player completely; it will compel the poorest passer on the opposing team to handle the ball and then force this poor passer into throwing the ball away; and it will completely control the offense of the opposing team.

Because it is an area press it can be strategically played to dominate the offense's patterns in that area. This means the defensive coach can determine his opponent's weakest offensive pattern and spring the press in that weak area.

The defense needs only to be taught in one area, then it can be expanded into all areas. But offenses must be learned for all areas because a team that uses only one offense to attack all areas finds that that offense does not work as well in all areas. An example: A full-court zone press attack does not work as well against a half-court zone press. So two offenses must be learned. A third offense must be learned for the three-quarter-court zone press. And a fourth for a face-guard zone press. And so on. But only one defense needs to be learned, and then just expand it. The wise coach finds the weakest offensive area and then attacks it.

Chapter 1 describes the basics of the press—the numbering system for the area and the numbering system of the tactic to be used. The entire press is described succinctly, yet completely, in the first chapter.

Chapter 2 provides the drills and fundamentals necessary to teach the press. This chapter also helps you determine where to press and whom to press. The all-out press is covered, and the safety press is explained.

Chapters 3 through 6 describe the press in the five areas of the court. It is in these chapters that you learn what works best against which players in which areas. Detailed coaching points are offered.

Chapter 7 teaches combinations that allow you to trap in more than one spot per possession, much like zone presses. This chapter also details how to develop a defensive game plan as well as how to adjust this plan from the bench during the game.

Every coach knows there are players who can be easily pressed and those who cannot. This press allows the defensive coach to force those players who can be pressed into handling the ball. Then a trap is set to steal the dribble or the pass.

Every coach also knows there are areas on the court where his team is not as efficient offensively as in other areas of the court. This adjustable area press allows the defensive coach to identify the weakest offensive area of the opposition. Then the press is applied there to compel even more turnovers.

The adjustable area press changes from man to zone and back to man every time a trap is set. So the offense attacking this press must change from a man press offense to a zone press offense, then back to a man press offense.

To solve this press completely, the offense must be efficient in three programs: They must have five excellent ballhandlers; the team offensive patterns must be solid at all areas of the court; and the offense must have the ability to change from a man offense to a zone offense, then back to a man offense. Any weakness in any of the three programs will be exploited by the adjustable area press.

Because the adjustable area press can be run the entire game—adjusting from attacking one player to attacking another, adjusting from attacking in one area to attacking in another area without giving up any layups (safety press)—it becomes an impossible maze for any attack to escape. And you will find strategies, how to teach the press, and all the little coaching details inside the next seven chapters.

Teams that play half-court defense for any period of time find their opponents adjusting and scoring almost every possession. Teams that pressure force more turnovers. These two facts alone dictate that the defensive coach teach a defense which compels turnovers and reduces the offensive efficiency of its opponents. This reduction of offensive efficiency and forcing of turnovers will lead to victory. Hence the need for the ADJUSTABLE AREA PRESS.

Chapter 1

How to Teach the Basics

Defenders need to exploit and dominate attackers, otherwise the advantage belongs to the offense. You can develop a defensive system that will accomplish this exploitation and domination; but in developing such a system, you must guard against complexity. A complex defense would confuse defenders, robbing them of spontaneous reactions. A simple aggressive defensive system is best.

The adjustable area press is a simple aggressive defense, yet it can seem quite complex to an attacking opponent. This chapter outlines how simple the numbering system is, yet how complex the press appears to the attackers.

FIRST NUMBER DESCRIBES
THE COURT MARKERS

Two numbers are used to call the press. The first number describes the area of the court, and the second number names the defensive tactic. For example, "37" would call for a trap to occur from a weakside wing defender (a "7" tactic) as the dribbler crosses the thirty area of the court. All defenders know and anticipate this. In anticipating this, all defenders begin to cheat in the direction of their coverage as the ball nears the thirty court marker (Diagram 1-1).

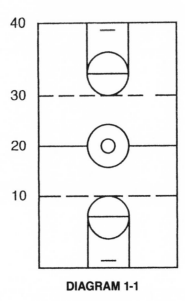

DIAGRAM 1-1

Diagram 1-1 displays the court markers. Any call in the "40's" puts the pressure defense into operation as the ball is thrown inbounds. Thirty-something calls compel the team defense into action as the ball crosses an imaginary line just above the top of the key on the far end of the court. This does not have to be an imaginary line. Because volleyball has become a team sport in all states, there is usually a volleyball line you can use as your thirty line. Anytime we are visiting for a game we look for a thirty line as we enter the gym. The twenty-something line is the midcourt line. The ten-something line is the three-point arc line. And the inside-the-ten line is just that—inside the three-point arc line.

SECOND NUMBER NAMES
THE DEFENSIVE TACTIC

While the first number dictates the area of the court where the team defensive strategy will occur, the second number names the tactic itself. There are ten digits, so we teach ten tactics. All do not have to be taught early in the season. But once taught, the tactic has year-to-year carryover value. The ten tactics are listed below. Each has a section of explanation devoted to describing the tactic itself. Chapter 2 provides the drills necessary to teach the tactic. Chapter 2, together with Chapters 3 through 7, expands on strategies to be used.

The Ten Tactics

These ten tactics, when used interchangeably and strategically, will completely confuse and disrupt any attack. That's the adjustability of the press. You will be shown how and when to make these strategic decisions.

- "0" names playing straight pressure man to man.
- "1" names a designated trap with named ball movement.
- "2" names a two-man run and jump.
- "3" names a three-man run and jump.
- "4" names a hedge and recovery.
- "5" names trapping the first pass receiver after the ball is advanced beyond the named court marker.
- "6" names trapping the dribbler from straight on.
- "7" names trapping the dribbler from the weakside.
- "8" names denying a designated attacker the ball and trapping when he gets the ball.
- "9" names trapping with a designated trapper by pass or by dribble.

"0"

"0" names playing straight pressure man-to-man defense.
To begin teaching the press, divide the full-court length into three lanes: the right lane, the middle lane, and the left lane. The middle lane should be drawn about three feet outside the foul lanes and extended from end line to end line (Diagram 1-2).

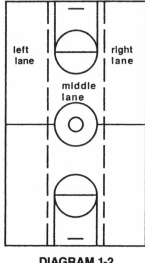

DIAGRAM 1-2

The Eight Principles

The press and the half-court defense have the same eight principles. These eight principles are listed below; all are taught by a single drill. (See "A Drill to Teach the Calls" later in this chapter.) You may teach your press and/or your half-court defense from any area. In this book, except for Chapters 3 through 7, all drills are discussed from different areas, so you can get a real feel for the press.

The eight principles are:

1. Pressure on the ball.

2. Denial on any attacking downcourt pass.

3. Jump to the ball.

4. One step off-line with the ball.

5. Deny flash pivot into the middle lane.

6. Close-out to the pass receiver.

7. Close-out to the dribbler.

8. Overplay the post in the middle lane.

Each of the above eight is discussed in the order given. The next section, "Drilling the "O" Principles," offers an eight-point drill you can use to teach the entire "O" defense in one drill.

1. Pressure on the ball

You cannot press if any defender refuses to put pressure on the ball. An attacker with the ball can spot open teammates down the court unless he is being pressured hard. Your team tactics will not work unless the ball is compelled to move at a reasonable rate. Without pressure, a point guard will merely walk the ball down the court. A pressure-on-the-ball drill is covered in Chapter 2 in the section "One-on-One Control." Individual techniques are discussed fully in that section.

2. Denial on any attacking downcourt pass

Attacking downcourt passes occur when the ball moves from one area marker to the next. Diagram 1-3 shows 3 with the ball trying to pass to 2. For the purpose of this drill, 2 can only break up and down the right lane, venturing sometimes into the middle lane. X2 must learn to cover 2 so 2 cannot receive the pass from 3.

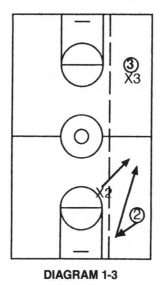

DIAGRAM 1-3

DRILL

(Diagram 1-3)

Objectives:

    1. To teach X3 to put pressure on the ball.

    2. To teach X2 to deny 2 the attacking downcourt pass.

Procedure:

1. To accomplish this pressure, X3 keeps his hands in the plane of the ball. If 3 raises the ball, X3's hands raise and his body becomes more in a stand-up position, with knees flexed but against 3's body. While in this position, 3 can only throw the pass. If 3 lowers the ball, X3 lowers his hands, takes a step back from 3, and bends more at the waist with greater knee flexion. When 3 lowers the ball, he now has the option of driving with the ball. For the purpose of this drill, 3 has been told he has already dribbled and picked up his dribble.

2. To accomplish this denial, X3 keeps his knees flexed and his body turned slightly toward 3. X2's right foot should be slightly behind his left foot. This enables X2 to see 3's eyes (X2 reads 3's eyes) and to see 2. X2 knows he has the sideline to help him. X2 knows his teammate X3 has his hands in the plane of the ball. This stance by X3 impels 3 to throw a lob or a bounce pass (both are slow passes, easily stolen). A careless attempt by 3 will be deflected by X3.

3. X2 wants to force the overhead lob by playing two-thirds the distance from the ball to his man. So as 2 fakes away, X2 takes only two steps for every three steps 2 takes.

4. Rotate from X3 to X2 to 2 to 3. Continue the drill until all players play all four positions.

3. Jump to the ball

Every defender must move in the direction of any pass; otherwise his assignment would cut between the ball and himself. A quick return pass to this cutter would break the press.

DRILL

(Diagram 1-4)

Objectives:

1. To teach X3 to jump to the ball on any pass thrown by his man, 3.

2. To teach X2 to adjust by closing out to the pass receiver (basic principle 6, discussed below).

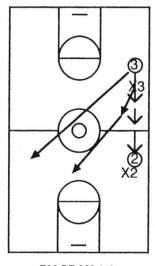

DIAGRAM 1-4

Procedure:

1. If X2 steals the attacking downcourt pass, the defense changes to offense immediately. But the worst thing X3 can do is turn to offense immediately by assuming X2 will intercept the pass. X3 must not only drop his right foot, staying low, swinging his body to see the completion of the pass to 2 (or the interception by X2), but X3 should also slide a few steps toward 2. This movement compels 3 to cut behind X3, leaving X3 in the perfect position between the ball, 2, and the new receiver, 3.

2. If X2 has better than a fifty percent chance for an interception, X2 goes for it. If X2 decides 2 is in a better position to receive the pass, X2 closes out to the new receiver (see basic principle 6 below).

4. One step off-line with the ball

By playing one step off-line with the ball, a weakside defender can offer help to a strongside defender. Also, this one step off-line of the ball prevents a direct pass to an offensive weakside attacker (only a lob pass can be thrown). This lob pass can be deflected, or certainly the defender can close-out to the weakside attacker as he receives the lob pass (see basic principle 6, discussed below).

DRILL

(Diagram 1-5)

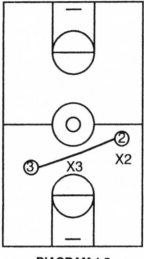

DIAGRAM 1-5

Objectives:

1. To teach the jump-to-the-ball defensive maneuver.
2. To teach the one-step-off-line-with-the-ball defensive technique.
3. To teach the closing-out-to-the-pass principle.

Procedure:

1. 3 passes to 2 and tries to break between X3 and the ball. X3 jumps to the ball to prevent this.
2. 2 tosses the ball toward 3 as 3 cuts. X3 deflects this pass, recovers it, and tosses the ball back to 2.
3. After 3 has reached weakside position, 2 rolls the ball toward 3. X3 catches this roll with both hands and dribbles down the floor a few dribbles before passing back to 2.
4. 2 throws a line-drive pass to 3. X3 steps into the passing lane for interception. X3 dribbles a step or two, then passes back to 2.

5. 2 throws a lob pass. X3 must judge if he can intercept. If X3 feels he can intercept this pass, he should be encouraged to do so. If X3 feels he cannot intercept this pass, he should close-out to the pass (see basic principle 6 below).

6. X2 puts pressure on the ball while 2 is throwing each of the four possible passes to the cutter, 3: the quick pass to the cutter, the bounce (roll) pass, the direct-line-drive pass, and the lob pass.

7. X2 must pressure the passer by constantly adjusting his feet and his hands as the passer moves the ball.

8. Rotate from 3 to X3 to 2 to X2 so all players can play each position.

5. Deny flash pivot into the middle lane

Defenders must never allow a direct pass into the middle lane. Weakside cutters who flash into the middle lane must be denied the pass. This means defenders on weakside attackers must have a proper beginning position, so they can beat the attacker to the spot on the floor in the middle lane. That proper position is one step off-line of their assignment and the ball and two-thirds the distance from the ball to their assignment. From this position the defender can easily deny a flash pivot cutter the ball.

DRILL

(Diagram 1-6)

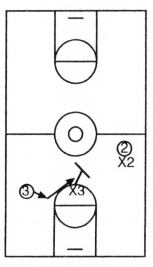

DIAGRAM 1-6

Objectives:

1. To learn the technique of denying flash pivot into the middle lane.
2. To learn to play one step off-line with the ball.
3. To learn to begin at two-thirds the distance from the ball.
4. To learn to pressure the ballhandler as the ballhandler adjusts the position of the ball.

Procedure:

1. 3 flashes toward 2 by dipping, then breaking, into the middle lane. X3 denies this flash by beginning in the proper position, then body-checking 3 as 3 moves toward the ball. This body checking is a legal bump by X3. X3 moves into 3's path, forcing 3 to change direction.
2. If 3 should receive a pass from 2, X3 must contain 3 for a moment or so, forcing a dribbling 3 into either the right or the left lane.
3. Rotate from 2 to X2 to X3 to 3, so each player can play each position.

6. Close-out to the pass receiver

Unfortunately, many more passes are completed than are stolen or deflected. Teaching how to close-out to these new pass receivers is of paramount importance. Proper close-out techniques prevent rapid advancement of the ball.

A defender wants to close-out to the new pass receiver with aggressive caution, but the defender wants to arrive as the ball arrives. The defender wants to get as close to the new receiver as possible, maybe even bumping the new receiver slightly. The defender wants to overplay the new receiver so the new receiver will have to dribble toward the nearest sideline.

The defender should be low, tail down, feet moving in a choppy motion. The defender's hands and arms should be aggressively slapping at the ball, compelling the new receiver to keep the ball high. The last step of the defender is a short, quick slide step. As the receiver brings the ball down, the defender backs off, shading the inside, impelling the attacker to dribble toward the outside lane. This forced dribbling to the outside takes the attacker on the longer route downcourt, allowing recovery time for other defenders. It also gives defenders the outside boundary lines as helpers should another trap be called.

7. Close-out to the dribbler

There are three types of closing-out to the dribbler: (a) to stop the breakaway dribbler, (b) to help a teammate recover on his own assignment, and (c) to stop the dribbler who has split the trap. Defenders must learn all three techniques.

a. To stop the breakaway dribbler. This usually happens when a defender tries for an interception but fails. The attacker receiving the ball becomes a breakaway dribbler, driving hard toward the basket. The defender nearest the breakaway dribbler on the side of the court where the dribble is occurring moves slowly toward the dribbler. The defender stays low and under control. The last few steps become short, quick slide steps, shading the inside, compelling the attacking dribbler to go the long route—the outside lanes. Teammates of this defender hustle to the basket area before regrouping.

b. To help a teammate recover on his assignment. This maneuver occurs often in a game. Because defenders must pressure the ball, these defenders often get beat on a first step and a dribble begins (Diagram 1-7). As 2 drives down the sideline, X3 takes a step or two toward 2. 2 does not know if a trap is about to occur; hence, 2 will usually slow his dribble. A hustling X2 can recover onto 2 while X3 hustles back to his assignment. To accomplish this technique successfully, X3 would want to get his body between 2 and 3, appearing big, with hands and arms outside his body and waving. 2 might, if he has been trapped a few times, pick up his dribble, thinking another trap might be appearing. X3 wants to be sure 2 does not successfully pass to 3. Appearing big and stepping toward 2 while retreating toward 3 will accomplish this. But if 2 merely slows his dribble, X2 can recover.

c. To stop the dribbler who splits the trap. Chapter 2 covers how to defense a dribbler who splits the trap and begins a dribble. This dribble should always be stolen by alert defenders. As you

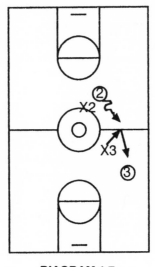

DIAGRAM 1-7

will see in Chapter 2, there will be a defender on both sides of this dribbler. This dribbler will either pick up the dribble, or the defender on the side of the dribble will flip it away. (See Chapter 2, "Stealing from Behind," for more details.)

8. Overplay the post in the middle lane

This axiom not only applies to the middle lane, but it also relates to the low post area (actually in the middle lane inside the ten area). The ball must be kept out of the middle and out of the low post. The proper defensive positioning is to front the post and watch the eyes of the passer while feeling with the hands and arms for the post attacker. If the post attacker is in the thirty or forty area, the defender can play slightly ballside with his body in a slight turn toward the post player. This allows the defender to quickly view any movement by the post. If the post is inside the ten area, the defender should maintain a full fronting position.

This complete overplay of the post should be the standard; however, there are times when the defense might want to trap the post (the post might be a very poor passer or a great scorer, for example). Trapping the post is covered in a section in Chapter 7.

DRILLING THE "0" PRINCIPLES

The eight principles discussed earlier comprise not only the defense inside the ten area, but also the "0" part of the full-court press. Each principle should be drilled separately until the techniques are mastered.

THE EIGHT-POINT DRILL

(Diagram 1-8)

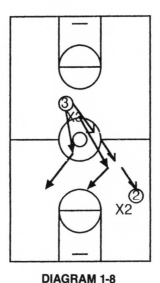

DIAGRAM 1-8

This eight-point drill can be used daily from different areas of the court as a review and a reminder of perfect "0" defense. Diagram 1-8 is used from the thirty area to show the drill. You should use the area from which you expect to apply the press the most or the area where you expect to play it the most in your next game.

Objectives:

1. To teach pressure on the ball.
2. To teach denial of any attacking downcourt pass.
3. To teach the defense to jump to the ball on passes.

4. To teach weakside defenders to play one step off-line with the ball and their assignment.

5. To teach denial of flash pivot into middle lane.

6. To teach proper close-out-to-pass-receiver techniques.

7. To teach closing-out to the dribbler.

8. To teach an overplay of any player posting in the middle lane.

Procedure:

1. X3 pressures 3 while X2 denies 2 the downcourt pass. 3 should be covered by X3 in an overplay to force 3 down the sideline if he chooses to dribble. For the purpose of this drill, 2 remains in the right outside lane. If 3 dribbles, X2 must close-out to the dribble. Proper denial techniques must be used by X2, and proper pressure techniques must be used by X3.

2. When 3 completes a pass to 2, X2 assumes proper pressure-on-the-ball technique (see earlier section, this chapter).

3. 3 now cuts, trying to get between X3 and the ball. X3 jumps to the ball.

4. Now you can let the drill continue live, in which case 2 makes a choice to dribble or to pass to 3. Or you can cover the four possible passes to 3 before letting the drill go live. The four passes are:

   a. Quick pass to the cutting 3, defended by X3 jumping to the ball;

   b. Bounce pass to 3, defended by X3 being one step off-line with the ball and two-thirds the distance from the ball;

   c. Line-drive pass to 3, defended by X3 being one step off-line with the ball and two-thirds the distance from the ball;

   d. Lob pass crosscourt to 3, defended by X3 moving back into 3 for the interception or by X3 using proper closing-to-the-pass techniques.

5. After drilling on these four passes, you can let the drill continue live. Or you can require 3 to flash pivot to the middle, defended by X3 using proper denial-of-the-flash-pivot techniques.

6. After drilling on denial of the flash pivot, you can let the drill continue live. Or you can allow 3 to post up in the middle lane, defended by X3 using proper overplay-the-post technique.

7. Anytime the drill becomes live, 2 has his dribble as well as the pass. X3 must, should 2 dribble, close-out to the dribbler using proper judgment and techniques.

8. Rotate from 3 to X3 to 2 to X2 so each player will know how to apply these eight cardinal principles of pressing.

ALTERNATIVE EIGHT-POINT DRILL

(Diagrams 1-9 and 1-10)

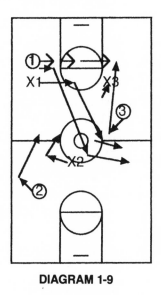

DIAGRAM 1-9

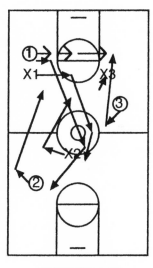

DIAGRAM 1-10

An alternative method of using the drill: You play as player 2. From the 2 position you can dictate which part of the drill you want to run.

When players begin to execute the eight points at a high level, you should begin with a three-on-three live set. Diagrams

1-9 and 1-10 show some of the options that might occur from a live three-on-three scrimmage. With only three defenders, you should easily see any mistakes and correct them immediately. You will be only as good as the decisions made by each defender.

Objectives:

1. To teach pressure on the ball.
2. To teach denying any downcourt passes.
3. To teach jumping to the ball as a pass is made.
4. To teach one step off-line with ball and assignment.
5. To teach denying flash pivot into the middle lane.
6. To teach closing-out to the pass receiver.
7. To teach closing-out to the dribbler.
8. To teach overplaying posting in the middle lane.

Procedure:

1. 3 faked X3 and received a pass from 1. X1 jumped to the ball and is now in complete denial of 1. 1 could have cut to the weakside instead of the strongside (Diagram 1-9).
2. X1's jump to the ball should have forced 1's cut behind X1. This kept X1 between the ball and his assignment.
3. Both X1 and X2 should be playing proper off-the-ball defense: X2 on the weakside and X1 on the strongside.
4. Diagram 1-10 shows 1 passing to 3 and cutting weakside. Now X1 is playing the weakside. 3 can pass the ball to 1 as 1 cuts. X1 must steal this pass by jumping to the ball. X3 puts pressure on the ballhandler, 3.
5. After 1 breaks to the weakside, he can flash pivot back to the middle lane. X1 must deny this flash pivot.
6. While in the middle lane, 1 could try to post X1. X1 must overplay this posting.
7. 3 could drive toward either X1 or X2 at any time. Whichever way 3 drives, the defender 3 is driving toward must close-out to the dribbler.

There are, of course, unlimited options available in this three-on-three shell game. The options presented represent only a few. However, the principles stay the same, and the axioms of the "0" defense must be mastered first.

After all players have mastered these eight principles, the trapping and strategic segments of the press can be taught. But the trapping and strategic segments should not be taught until the "0" parts of the press are learned well. The "0" part can be drilled separately as needed during the season, or the "0" part can be reviewed and taught daily by use of the eight-point drill.

"1"

"1" names a designated trap with the first ball movement.

Whenever the last digit is "1," such as "41," it means a trap with the first ball movement. This is a frequent call when the offensive team likes to get the ball into a point guard, then clear out all the point guard's teammates. While the point guard holds the ball, the defenders go with their assignments up to about the half-court line, staying in denial position. When the point guard starts his first dribble, the wing defender on the side away from the dribble begins immediately to race back toward this point guard to set the trap (for trapping techniques, see Chapter 2). The defender on the point guard forces a change in direction, and the trap is set. Now five or six of the ten seconds have elapsed. A pass out of the trap takes another second or two. And proper close-out to the new pass receiver will frequently result in a ten-second violation call if the pass is not intercepted.

Of if the point guard holds the ball for his teammates to clear out and a few run and jumps have already occurred during the ball game, the point guard will spin-dribble out of what he perceives as another run and jump. Now a trap coming from the weakside would almost assure a ten-second violation. It would take that long for the point guard to advance the ball against two defenders (trappers).

Or you could run combinations (see Chapter 7). The call could be "42" into "37." "42" calls for a two-man run and jump. "37" asks for a trap from the weakside wing. This means the attacking point guard faces a two-man run and jump followed by trapping by two defenders. (For more details, see Chapter 7.)

"2"

"2" names a two-man run and jump.

Diagram 1-11 shows "42." The ball has been inbounded to 1. X1 has forced 1 to the outside lane, then overplayed 1. 1 must change direction or charge X1. As 1 changes direction, X3 and X1 implement the two-man run and jump. X3 must go directly in the line between 1 and 3, making his body big by raising his arms. If 1 has been trapped a few times previously, 1 might pick up the dribble. X1 hurries back into the passing lane between 1 and 3. X1 and X3 have switched assignments.

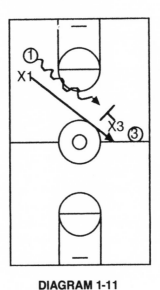

DIAGRAM 1-11

Diagram 1-12 displays the two-man run and jump down the sideline. The same coaching techniques are used. X1 forces 1 to change direction. X3 runs directly at 1, appearing big, but under control. X1 hustles back into the passing lane between 1 and 3. X1 and X3 exchange assignments.

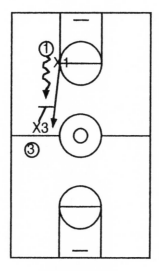

DIAGRAM 1-12

"3"

"3" names a three-man run and jump.

Diagram 1-13 represents a three-man run and jump. X1 forces 1 into the left outside lane before compelling 1 to change direction. As this change of direction occurs, X2 races toward 1. 1 is not sure if this is a trap, a hedge and recover (see the "4" section), or a run and jump. 1 may hesitate, which helps the defense. X3 leaves 3 at the exact moment X2 left 2. X3 looks for the "habit" pass, which is the one most often made. The habit pass is a direct pass to the player whose defender has just left. 1 sees X2 leave 2, so the habit pass would be to 2. X1 circles back to cover 3. All three defenders have exchanged assignments: X2 is on 1 even if he continues dribbling, X3 covers 2, and X1 defends 3. The press continues.

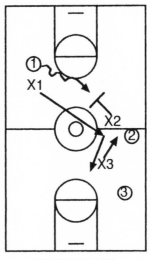

DIAGRAM 1-13

"4"

"4" names a hedge and recover.

There are two types of hedge and recoveries: (1) violent rush and (2) soft rush. A dribbling guard who does not want to pick up the dribble and pass should see the violent rush. This violent rush gives the impression of a trap about to occur, compelling the dribbling guard to pick up his dribble. But a dribbling guard who picks up his dribble and passes quickly should experience the soft rush. The soft rush gives the defender time to recover to his own assignment for the interception. His distance back to his assignment is very short. A step or two with exaggerated fakes illustrates the soft rush, while the violent rush is a hard three or four steps toward the dribbler before recovering.

"5"

"5" names trapping the first pass receiver after the ball is advanced beyond the named court area.

"25," therefore, would name a trap of the first pass receiver after the ball crosses the half-court line (the twenty area). "25" is our call. Diagram 1-14 illustrates "25" and all "5" calls.

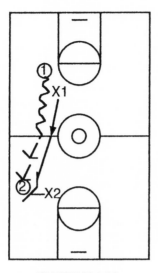

DIAGRAM 1-14

1 is dribbling toward the midcourt line (Diagram 1-14). X1 is pressuring 1 but trailing slightly so 1 will not change his direction (it will not change the defense even if 1 does change direction). X2 plays off 2, showing 1 the open passing lane to 2. X2 should be facing 1 and slightly below a line through 2 parallel to the baseline. This encourages 1 to pass to 2. It also discourages 1 from driving hard because X2 is in perfect help position. This is the only time the downcourt defender is not between the ball and his assignment. But any "5" calls means a trap on the new pass receiver. So the downcourt defender would want to encourage the pass to his assignment by playing off his assignment. X2 would deny 2 any pass until the ball nears the called court area (in this case, twenty—the midcourt line).

Once the ball is passed to 2, X2 immediately puts the trap on 2 (for details on trapping procedures, see Chapter 2), not allowing 2 to drive toward the middle lane and not allowing 2 to escape to his right with a dribble (Diagram 1-14). X1 immediately races to help X2 trap. Once X1 arrives, X2 and X1 get against 2, bumping him with their thighs, but not allowing 2 to split between X1 and X2.

Regardless of the direction in which 2 decides to dribble, X1 and X2 maintain the trap. These defenders need to stay within six feet of the dribbler (closely guarded position). After five seconds, this is a violation, giving the defense the ball. 2 knows this and will frequently rush the pass, giving the interceptors an opportunity for a steal. (See Chapter 2 for interceptor's coverage rules.)

"6"

"6" names trapping the dribbler from straight on.

"26" is our call. Diagram 1-15 illustrates "26" and all "6" calls.

X1 pressures the ball hard (Diagram 1-15). X1 does not care if 1 changes direction. The trap will occur from straight on. So if 1 changes direction to the right lane instead of to the left lane, the defender in that lane will trap straight on. The trapper is the wing defender in the same lane when 1 crosses the half-court line.

X2 plays between the ball and 2, discouraging the direct pass. X2 has his left leg slightly behind his right leg, but X2's body is in the passing lane between 1 and 2. This discourages the pass from 1 to 2 (Diagram 1-15). X2 can be faking toward 1 and retreating, like it was a hedge-and-recover call, before racing to trap. This just gives 1 another worry, compelling 1 to be more defensive in his attack.

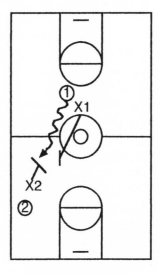

DIAGRAM 1-15

As 1 dribbles across the half-court line (the "20" call), X2 races toward 1 to help X1 set the trap on 1 (Diagram 1-15). All of the interceptors know when the trap is to be sprung, so they have been cheating toward their interceptors' posts as 1 nears crossing the half-court line.

X1's pressure on 1 should prevent 1 from spotting an open receiver immediately. Also 1's habit pass would be to 2, because 1 can see X2 leaving 2 (see Chapter 2 for coverage of this habit pass). Defense of the habit pass should be covered and drilled daily. This lane should be covered first and quickly by an interceptor (see Chapter 2 for drills and coverage rules).

X1 and X2 stay and trap 1 until the ball is passed. If 1 chooses to keep his dribble alive, X1 and X2 stay within six feet (closely guarded distance); within five seconds, the defense has caused a turnover.

It is easy to see how this trap can be effective late in the game when a run and jump ("22" or "23") or hedge and recovery ("24") has been called during the game. 1 can easily become confused, hesitant, and defensive-minded. This attitude by 1 creates even more turnovers, disrupts the offensive team patterns and timing, and often compels 1 to pick up his dribble when he should not and keep his dribble alive when he should not.

"7"

"7" names trapping the dribbler from the weakside (this requires forcing the dribbler into a change of direction).

"27" is our call. Diagram 1-16 illustrates "27" and all "7" calls.

Where the "6" calls mean we will trap the dribbler coming straight on, the "7" calls mean the defender on the ball must force a change of direction at or near the called area marker. In Diagram 1-16, X1 pushes 1 outside into the left lane, then X1 compels 1 to change directions by overplaying 1's dribble. X2, the outside right-lane defender, knows when this change of direction will occur. X2 stays in the passing lane between his man and the ball. X2 races hard toward 1, hoping to reach 1 just as he comes out of his spin move. X1 and X2 continue with the trap until 1 passes the ball. If 1 chooses to continue his dribble, X1 and X2 continue to trap.

Teammates of X1 and X2 race hard to their interceptor

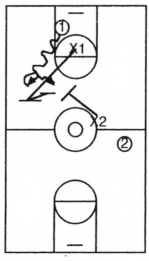

DIAGRAM 1-16

positions. They cheat to their coverage areas because they know by the call ("27") where and when the trap will occur. The habit passing lane would be to 2, and this lane must be covered first.

It is very easy to see how 1 would become completely confused and very hesitant when faced with the run and jump, traps from straight on, traps from changes of direction, and hedges and recoveries. And when these come from different areas of the court, it becomes too much for even a great player to overcome.

No offensive team can devise patterns to attack all ten of your options, much less five different spots on the floor. You, the coach, can determine where the opposition's attack is weakest. Springing all ten defensive tactics (or a few, your choice) will cause turnovers galore and completely disrupt your opponent's well-timed offensive machine. (See Chapter 2 for ideas on discovering where the opponent's attack is weakest.)

"8"

"8" names denying a designated attacker the ball and trapping when he gets it back.

If "48" is the call, you can double-team the designated attacker before the ball is inbounded.

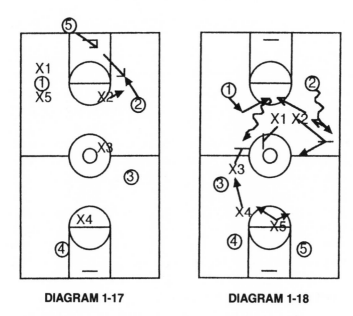

DIAGRAM 1-17   **DIAGRAM 1-18**

"48" is our call. Diagrams 1-17 and 1-18 illustrate "48" and all "8" calls.

In Diagram 1-17, we have designated 1, the opponent's point guard, as the attacker we do not want to handle the ball. X1 and X5 double-team 1 to compel the pass into another player. The defender on the other player could play soft to encourage the pass into the other player. We could then play the straight "0" defense until 1 gets open to receive a pass; or we could play for another trap as the weaker ballhandler tries to bring the ball up the floor. Once 1 receives a pass, we double-team him on his first dribble. 1 is simply not going to be allowed to bring the ball up the floor.

If 2, in Diagram 1-17, is a poor ballhandler, you would want to run a trap, such as "36." 2 would possibly turn the ball over many times during the course of a game. But running "36" instead of staying straight "0" would make it easier for your opponents to get the ball back to 1. This is a tough decision a coach must make.

Let's say the ball has moved upcourt from Diagram 1-17 to Diagram 1-18 and 1 has freed himself for a pass from 2. Now when 1 makes his first move to dribble the ball, a straight-on double-team will occur. Diagram 1-18 shows 1 dribbling toward the left sideline. X3 comes to trap. X2, X4, and X5 move to their interception spots.

Because 1 is double-teamed before the pass is inbounded (Diagram 1-17), the passer, 5, will usually throw the pass inbounds to 2, the line of least resistance. This helps keep the ball out of 1's hands. That's the purpose of "8" calls—to keep the ball out of a particular player's hands.

When you dictate who you are going to trap, you choose a weaker passer and dribbler. This weaker passer and dribbler will turn over the ball almost at will. (For these strategies and how you select them, see Chapter 2.)

You should always limit the effectiveness of the opposition's star player(s). You decide who to limit and where to make that limitation. For example, a great dribbling point guard who cannot shoot can break the press but is totally ineffective near the basket area. So you would want to "48" or "38" the point guard, then play completely off him in the ten area. A great post player, on the other hand, would experience "18" and never see "48" or "38." In fact, if the great point guard was a non-shooter, you might want to double-team the great post player with the defensive point guard—a "19" call, as you will see in the next section.

"9"

"9" names trapping with a designated trapper.

"39" is our call. Diagram 1-19 illustrates "39" and all "9" calls.

Let's say the opponent's big man, 5 in Diagram 1-19, cannot dribble the ball and does not have good hands. X5 can become the designated trapper. X5 cheats upcourt after the ball has been inbounded. X1 pressures 1. X1 does not care in which direction 1 begins his dribble, but X1 wants to keep 1 going in that direction once he does begin. This keys the off-the-ball defenders, the interceptors, where to go and when to make their moves to the interceptors' spots.

As 1 begins his dribble, X5 races upcourt to help X1 trap 1 as 1 crosses the court-area mark. The interceptors hustle to their interceptors' spots.

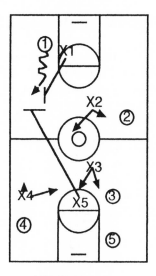

DIAGRAM 1-19

It is easy to see how effective this tactic can be after 1 has faced the run and jump, the traps ("45," "46," "47"), and the hedges. Each of these strategies contributes to the others by confusing the ballhandler. Each of these tactics leaves a different attacker open momentarily—the habit pass. Now the attacker left open is the farthest away from the double-team. An adequate double-team almost assures a turnover or two, a two- to four-point turnaround. Many games are won by smaller margins.

A "9" call, for example, would have the designated trapper trapping inside the three-point arc. Let's say the opponents have a great-scoring post player but a weak-shooting perimeter player. The designated trapper would be the player guarding the poor-shooting perimeter player. And every time the great-scoring post player received a pass, the designated trapper and the post's defender would trap this great post player. This strategy, called "9," would reduce the great-scoring post player as a threat. The "9" call in this instance would be trapping the post anytime he receives the ball.

DRILLING THE CALLS

You want to drill your press against the offensive sets of your next opponent, and you want this drilling to simulate actual game situations. Do this by using placards and not letting the offense see your calls.

A DRILL TO TEACH THE CALLS

(Diagram 1-20)

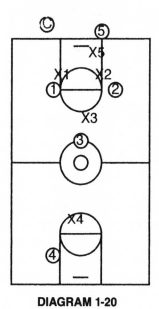

DIAGRAM 1-20

Objectives:

    1. To drill on the various calls. Use this to prepare your next game plan or to drill randomly on the calls.

    2. To teach players to transfer the calls into live defenses.

Procedure:

    1. Put five players on the court in your offensive set or the set of your next opponent.

    2. Have these five players face the opposite end of the court from the coach.

    3. Put defenders on each of the offensive players.

4. Coach has placards for numbers 0 through 49. Coach can choose just the ones he intends to use in the next ball game.

5. Defensive players watch the coach's signal. Offensive players look upcourt away from the coach. This allows the defense to know the call, and the offense must operate without knowing the call.

6. Coach passes the ball to 5 and the possession begins. If the defense steals a pass, they fast-break or set up to score.

7. If the offense scores, defensive players run their fast break then hustle to original positions and the drill begins again. Coach can allow the same defense to be in operation, or he can call a different one.

HOW TO MAKE THE NUMBERING SYSTEM WORK

You do not want to begin with all the tactics installed in your defensive system. You want to begin with only five.

Those five would include "0" and "4." "0" is your primary defense all over the floor, including half-court, so it must be included. "4" is very easily taught. To these you would want to add one of "1," "8," or "9." You would also want one run and jump, so teach either "2" or "3." Your fifth should include a trap from either "5," "6," or "7."

After teaching the basic five you want, include the other two traps—whichever two you did not include in your basic five—then put in the remaining three.

When you go to make your decision about the basic five, you should inspect your schedule; study the teams you play early. Do they have a great point guard? Do they have a superior post player? Do they, as a team, attack a press well? How good is the opposing coach at adjusting his team from the bench? All these questions will help you determine which of the ten tactics you want to teach first.

Your next decision is where to teach the tactics. You should begin your teaching of the tactics at half-court (the twenty area).

From this area it is easy to expand to thirty and forty. It is also easy to drop to ten or inside the ten.

Your next preseason planning will involve the combinations (see Chapter 7). Do you want just one trap per possession? Or do you want two traps? Do you want a tactic followed by a trap? After reading Chapter 7 and studying the different combinations, you may decide to use one or more. These combinations should be taught last.

All the fundamentals are the same. All the traps and interception coverage rules are the same. The tactics are different, but the ingredients that make up the tactics are the same (traps, rules, etc.). So once the fundamentals and drills of Chapter 2 are taught, the tactics are easily installed. You should begin teaching the fundamentals, the drills, and the rules on opening practice day. Then you can add the five tactics you want in five easy practice days. You should fix a calendar for when you want to install the others.

In Chapter 7 there is a section on how to prepare a game plan. The above discussion is for preseason planning.

Once you have used this system for a year, it has great carryover value. Whatever you have taught will be immediately available the next year. If you have a younger team in your program, such as a junior varsity team, you could teach them the "0," "4," "2," "3," "5," "6," and "7" calls. This would not only give your junior varsity a great press, but its carryover value to your varsity would allow you to put in the "1," "8," and "9" calls immediately.

Chapter *2*

How to Drill
the Fundamentals

Chapter 1 discussed the elements of the press—the numbering system, the tactics, and how to best apply them. Chapter 2 takes up the fundamentals and the basics.

Chapter 2 shows you how to set and maintain your traps. You will learn how a player controls his assignment one on one, how to steal the ball from behind, how to cover the passing lanes (coverage rules), how to run the all-out press as well as the safety press, and how to recover when a pass is successfully made out of the traps. There is also a section on how to pick the court markers, how to pick the tactics, how to pick the players to be trapped, and how to take advantage of the other team's patterns and tendencies.

ONE-ON-ONE CONTROL

Without a perfect beginning stance the defender will be at a great disadvantage; but with a good beginning stance, the defender has the upper hand. The defender who begins correctly controls his assignment.

Let's consider the stance from three perspectives: (1) after the attacker has received the pass but before he dribbles, (2) as the attacker dribbles, and (3) after the attacker picks up his dribble.

The defender should reach his assignment as he receives the pass. The defender should be against the attacker, compelling him to pause and to put the ball at least chest high. The defender should be flexed at the knees ready to retreat when the attacker brings the ball down. But as long as the ball remains in a high position the defender should wave his arms and get as close as possible to the attacker, maybe even bumping him. From this high ball position the attacker can only pass. The defender's hands should be in the same plane as the ball.

When the attacker pulls the ball down into a triple-threat position, he is ready to dribble. The defender now wants to retreat a step, still being able to touch the chest of the attacker with the palms of his hands, but retreating mentally, with feet moving. The defender wants to shade a half-body inside, compelling the attacker to dribble down the outside lane. This shade means the defender's front foot should be about a half-step behind the attacker. This trail foot should be slightly back from the front foot. The front foot should be nearer the sideline than the trail foot. The body should be wide, with the knees pointed outward. This should prevent the attacker from turning the corner on his dribble. It may even propel the dribbling attacker more toward the sideline, which is good for the press.

As the dribble continues, the defender must adjust his stance in accordance with the defensive tactic that has been called. If the tactic requires a change of direction, as the "7" calls do, the defender races hard, using quicker slide steps, to put his nose on the ball. The attacker can no longer continue without charging, so the attacker must change direction. The defender wants to time this nose-on-the-ball technique to correspond to the area where the tactic has been called (for example, "37" would be the thirty area).

If a straight-on tactic has been called, the defender would not want to give this away; so the defender pressures the attacker, staying very low, using hand fakes (in-and-out motion). Defenders on the ball must use quick slide steps, never crossing their legs. The defender wants to offer great pressure but not allow the attacker to drive free. The defender on the ball has help from his teammates. They constantly jab fake toward the dribbler before recovering on their own assignments (hedge and recover).

Should the attacker pick up his dribble before the tactic is set, the defender immediately gets against the dribbler-turned-passer, placing his hands in the plane of the ball, bumping the attacker ever so gently. Now the defender is in an almost vertical position.

When the ball is passed, the defender on the passer jumps to the ball and gets ready to deny the ball back to his man or to run whatever new tactic has been called. We teach this one-on-one control by use of a drill.

ONE-ON-ONE ZIGZAG-CONTROL DRILL
(Diagram 2-1)

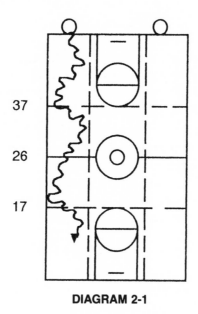

37

26

17

DIAGRAM 2-1

Objectives:

1. To teach attackers to free themselves with a dribble.

2. To teach defenders to control their assignments and still maintain adequate pressure.

3. To teach turning attackers at the exact and precise moment of a called tactic.

Procedure:

1. Line up players as shown in Diagram 2-1. Rotate from offense to defense to end of the line. Go down and back before rotating.

2. Divide the court into three lanes. The outside two are used simultaneously.

3. The dribbler the first time down and back does not try to escape, allowing the defender to get used to using the slide step, the swing step, and the drop step.

4. On the second trip down and back, the defender tries to force a change of direction every one-fourth court. On this trip the attacker should be trying to escape the defender.

5. On the third trip the defender should force the change of direction at the precise area of the court you called. For example, in our next game we intend to use "37," "26," and "17." This means a change of direction should be forced at the thirty area, no change of direction at the twenty area, and another change at the ten area. The attacker should not know where these changes will occur.

6. The slide step is used until there is a change in direction. As this change occurs, the defender drop-steps with the trail leg. This is known as the swing step. Now the defender's opposite leg is forward, and the defender is sliding in the opposite direction.

ONE-ON-ONE MULTIPLE-CONTROL DRILL
(Diagram 2-2)

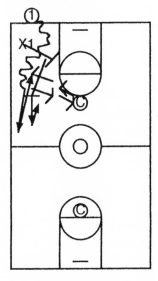

DIAGRAM 2-2

This drill allows development of control of the player dribbling the ball as well as passing the ball and trying to get open to get a pass.

Objectives:

1. To teach one-on-one control of the dribbler.
2. To teach jumping to the ball on a pass.
3. To teach denying the pass back to a downcourt attacker.
4. To teach closing-out to the new pass receiver.
5. To teach closing-out to a new dribbler.

Procedure:

1. Line up players as shown in Diagram 2-2. Rotate from 1 to X1 to end of line.
2. 1 dribbles as X1 runs the zigzag-control drill. After 1 gets the dribble above the first coach, he stops his dribble and passes to the first coach. 1 now tries to free himself for the pass back from the coach while X1 tries to deny this pass.
3. When 1 gets the pass from the first coach, the zigzag drill continues until 1 dribbles past the second coach. Now 1 tries to free himself from X1's denial maneuvers. When 1 gets the pass from the second coach, the drill continues in a zigzag form.
4. Player 1 is allowed to operate only in the left outside lane (or the right outside lane).

TRAPPING DRILLS
AND STANCES

Defenders must learn to trap in three situations: as an attacker continues dribbling, after an attacker picks up the dribble, and after an attacker receives a pass but before dribbling. Each requires a little different stance and coverage.

To cover a dribbler who is being trapped but refuses to pick up his dribble, the two defenders would want to stay within six feet of the dribbler. If this occurs in the front court, it would compel a violation after five seconds. If in the back court, a possible ten-second violation would occur if the two defenders can keep the dribbler from turning the corners. The defender on the left would prevent the attacker from turning the right corner, and the defender on the right would prevent the attacker from turning his left corner. Both would cover the middle.

If the dribbler escapes around a corner, the defender on that side must race to a cutoff position while his teammate races to stay as the second trapper. If the dribbler manages to split the trap, both defenders turn upcourt, racing alongside the attacker, trying to deflect the dribble if it is on their side. (More about this in "Stealing from Behind," the next section.)

Maintaining proper body position is important. The trappers on the dribbler want to have a slight flexion at the knee joints, grabbing the floor with their toes and maintaining enough distance between themselves and the dribbler so he cannot escape with the dribble. Both trappers stay with the dribbler until he passes the ball. (See the "Recovery" section later in this chapter for recovery positions.)

When the dribbler picks up the dribble, he has no means of escape. Both defenders immediately get against the attacker, bumping him ever so slightly. Both defenders keep their hands in the plane of the ball; their inside feet should meet at a ninety-degree angle, and their knees should cross.

If the trap is to be set on an attacker as he receives the pass, it must be remembered that the dribble is still a possibility. Nevertheless, both trappers want to race up against the body of the attacker, bumping him ever so slightly. The defenders want their hands in the plane of the ball and their feet at ninety-degree angles, trying to get the new pass receiver to keep the ball high and protected by the attacker's body. Should the attacker pull the ball down into a triple-threat position, the defenders immediately retreat a half-step, inviting the dribble. They stay with this attacker as long as he dribbles. The interceptors would make the adjustments.

BASIC TRAPPING DRILL

(Diagrams 2-3 and 2-4)

Objectives:

1. To teach trapping techniques.

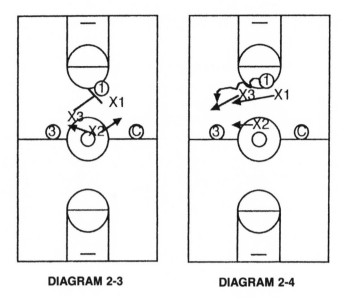

DIAGRAM 2-3　　　　**DIAGRAM 2-4**

2. To teach interceptors to cover two players.
3. To teach trappers to stay with the dribbler until the dribble is picked up.

Procedure:

1. Line up players as shown. Rotate from 1 to X1 to X2 to X3 to 3 to end of line.
2. Coach passes to 1 to begin the drill. You could allow 1 to dribble up to the area of the trap (thirty in this case).
3. X3 immediately races to trap with X1 (Diagram 2-3).
4. X2 covers a pass to 3 (habit pass) and a pass to the coach (Diagram 2-4).
5. We have a saying, "Walk to Contain—Race to Trap." X1 keeps 1 under control (walk to contain) while X3 comes hard to help trap (race to trap).
6. If 1 keeps the dribble live, X1 and X3 keep their coverage while X2 adjusts his interception angle. X2 shades the player in the direction of 1's dribble, hoping 1 will try to pass-cross his body, an easier pass to intercept.

TRAPPER DECISION DRILL

(Diagram 2-5)

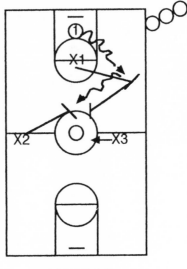

DIAGRAM 2-5

Objectives:

1. To teach trapping techniques.
2. To teach staying with the dribbler while the dribbler continues.
3. To teach decision making by the defender (who will the trapper be).

Procedure:

1. Line up players as shown in Diagram 2-5. Rotate from 1 to X1 to X2 to X3 to end of line. In the area press all defenders must be able to play all positions (a player never knows if his assignment will be bringing the ball up the court).
2. In Diagram 2-5, "37" has been the call. X1 forces 1 to change directions about the thirty marker. X2 races hard to help X1 trap 1. X3 becomes an interceptor. (See "Rules" later in this chapter.)

3. 1 must, during this drill, try to dribble the length of the court against two trapping defenders. The two trappers want to harass the dribbler with in-and-out fakes, stealing any unprotected dribble. If 1 splits the trappers, X1 and X2 race downcourt on their respective sides of 1, flicking the dribble from behind. (See the next section, "Stealing from Behind.")

4. If the call had been "36," X1 would not have turned 1 and X3 would have raced hard to help X1 trap 1.

5. You would want to move the trappers (X2 and X3) to the area where you intend to set the most traps in the next ball game.

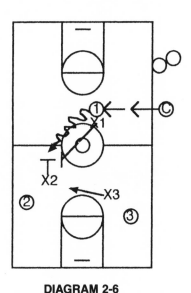

DIAGRAM 2-6

Let's use the "26" call to explain trapping straight on. Diagram 2-6 displays the same drill as Diagram 2-5, except it has been moved downcourt to the twenty area.

X2 and X3 both have to keep their assignments from receiving a pass. X1 must keep 1 under control, but X1 wants to force 1 out of the middle lane. As 1 approaches the twenty area, X2 races to trap with X1 (the call was "26," meaning the trap comes from straight on). X3 becomes an interceptor and slides into the middle lane. (See "Interceptor's Rules," later in this chapter.)

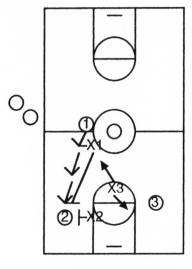

DIAGRAM 2-7

Diagram 2-7 shows the same drill as Diagram 2-5, except a different call, "25," is being discussed. "25" means the trap occurs on the first pass after the dribbler passes the twenty mark. X1 keeps 1 under control, impelling 1 to get out of the center lane. X2 and X3 play a sagging defense, encouraging 1 to pass to either 2 or 3. Once the pass is made, X2 keeps 2 from driving down the outside lane and from driving to the middle lane. X2 gets against 2 just as X1 arrives to help trap. X1 also bumps against 2. X3 becomes an interceptor.

STEALING FROM BEHIND

Our philosophy concerning pressure on the ballhandler before he dribbles is designed to impel the dribble. Hopefully that dribble will be a split of the trap. A dribbler who splits the trap must be dribbling with a defender on both sides. The defender on the side of the dribble is encouraged to flick the ball from behind toward a downcourt teammate. After a few flicks from behind, the dribbler who splits the trap will not dribble more than one or two dribbles for fear that the ball will be flicked. This fear aids the defense.

The flick begins with proper position on the attacker who receives the pass and before the attacker dribbles. Both defenders should be up against the attacker, bumping him, with knees flexed, toes grabbing the floor, and knees crossing each other.

This stance immediately discourages the split. But a fake by the attacker in either direction usually leads the attacker to use the step-through move and commence the dribble after splitting the defenders. When the attacker fakes around either corner (for discussion, let's fake the right corner), the defender on that side drops a step and shades the outside, preventing the attacker from dribbling around the corner. The defender's teammate slides to offer help.

Attackers are taught to make this fake, then step through (splitting the trap), bringing the ball low and commencing the dribble. This is exactly what we want them to do. The two defenders on the dribbler invite this step-through. Both defenders retreat a step and spread slightly. The attacker sees this and thinks he has split the trap. As the attacker begins his dribble, the defender on the side of the dribble flicks the ball downcourt. After a few flicks, the attacker will try to dribble around the corner (easier to maintain trapping position) instead of splitting the trap. This, too, aids the defense. This flicking maneuver is taught by the Flicking Drill.

FLICKING DRILL

(Diagram 2-8)

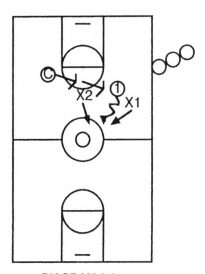

DIAGRAM 2-8

Objectives:

1. To teach trapping techniques.
2. To teach the offensive player to split the trap (step through).
3. To teach trappers to prevent the dribbler from dribbling around the corner.
4. To teach flicking the dribble if the trap is split.

Procedure:

1. Line up players as shown in Diagram 2-8. Rotate from 1 to X1 to X2 to end of line.
2. Coach begins the drill by passing to 1. 1 must dribble the ball the length of the court against two defenders.
3. X1 does not allow 1 to go to the right. X2 does not allow 1 to get around the left corner. If 1 splits the trap, the defender on that side anticipates this, goes with the dribbler, and flicks the dribble downcourt.

COVERING THE LANES

For coverage rules the court is divided into the strongside lane (where the trap is), the center lane, and the weakside lane. By varying the traps (off-pass, off-dribble, off-straight on, off-weakside) and varying the area (forty, thirty, twenty), the defenders gain the advantage. The coverage rules stay the same, yet the attacking offense must vary. Hence confusion results in the offensive attack, and attackers actually become defensive-minded in their attack.

Rules

With Center-Lane Attacker:

1. First defender down the strongside is a trapper.
2. First defender down the middle lane covers the habit pass as well as the middle.

3. First defender on the weakside covers the middle lane and the weakside.

4. Second defender in any lane (if he sees a center-lane attacker) covers the basket area.

Without Center-Lane Attacker:

1. First defender down the strongside is a trapper.

2. Second defender down the strongside covers the habit pass as well as the middle lane.

3. First defender on the weakside covers the middle lane as well as the weakside lane.

4. Second defender on the weakside (or third defender down the strongside) guards the basket area.

Keep in mind that the defense is man to man until the trap is set. As the trap is being set, interceptors race to their positions, creating an umbrella and a safety. In fact, interceptors should anticipate the trap and actually begin moving before the trap is set. As these interceptors race to their positions, they are actually moving into the primary passing lanes. This makes interceptions easier.

Careful inspection of the rules above displays simplicity. Both sets are actually the same, except one set does not have an attacker in the middle lane. Let's now study four popular sets and apply the rules. We will use "36" to explain each. This way it is the same press but different attacks. It is easy to see if the attack was successful against "36," the defensive coach could call "35" and completely take the offense out of its success. Yet the defensive rules would be the same.

Diagram 2-9 displays an offensive set with a middle-lane attacker. X5 can see this middle-lane attacker. X5 knows, therefore, that he is the second defender down the middle lane.

X1 keeps the pressure on 1, impelling 1 down the left-side lane. As 1 crosses the thirty-area mark, X2 races to help X1 trap 1. X4 knows that this trap will occur as 1 crosses the thirty marker, but 1 does not know this, giving X4 the advantage. X4, per his coverage rule, moves toward the habit pass to 2, the player left vacated when X2 left for the trap. X4 moves as X2 moves. They both move as 1 crosses the thirty area. X3, the weak-lane defender,

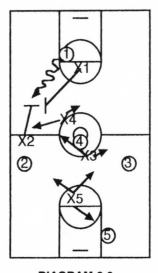

DIAGRAM 2-9

also leaves as 1 crosses the thirty mark. X3 races to cover the middle lane and the weakside lane. Once the trap is set, X5, the safety, can come several feet up the court to help out on any poorly thrown pass by 1. If 1 keeps his dribble live, the umbrella defenders, X4 and X3, stay between the attackers, reading the eyes of 1, gambling for the interception. X2 and X1 keep their hands in the plane of the ball, should 1 pick up his dribble.

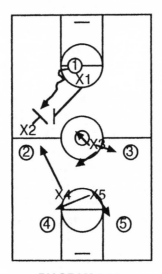

DIAGRAM 2-10

Diagram 2-10 exhibits the same press, but the attack does not have a center-lane player. The same rules apply. The same press is in effect.

As 1 dribbles across the thirty marker, X2 races to trap. X4 knows this and hurries to get into the habit passing lane, covering the strongside lane and the middle lane. X3 covers the middle lane and the weakside lane. X5 is again safety, guarding the basket.

Teams will not stay motionless against your press. They will move in hopes of confusing your defenders. But the press rules are activated as the attackers cross your marked area. The attackers do not know where this area is. By varying your area and your call, you keep the attack off-balance all night. They can only guess where to begin their movement.

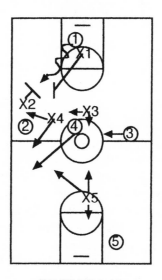

DIAGRAM 2-11

Diagram 2-11 shows the very popular diagonal cut to beat the press. 4 cuts diagonally as he sees the trap occurring. The same rules apply. X2 goes to help X1 trap 1 as 1 crosses the thirty area. 3 cuts into the middle lane as 3 sees the trap. X3 covers both the middle lane and the weakside lane. There is no player in the weakside lane so X3 can concentrate on the middle-lane player, 3. X3 still mentally covers the weakside lane as well as the middle lane, but X3 does not want to guard space. X4 immediately takes the habit pass to 2, but X4 also watches for the lob pass to 4. X5,

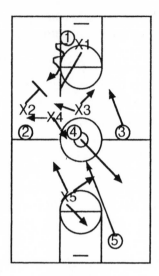

DIAGRAM 2-12

when the trap is set, can come upcourt to help on the carelessly thrown pass to 4. X5's major responsibility is to guard the basket.

Diagram 2-12 has 4 cutting to the weakside and 5 breaking from deep position to post up in the center lane. The coverage remains the same. X3 covers the weakside and the center lane. As long as 1 dribbles toward the right side, X3 would concentrate more on the center lane. X4 still covers the strongside lane (the habit pass) and the middle lane. This is because X4 was in the middle-lane coverage as 1 crossed the thirty area (the call was "36"). X5 yells to let the defenders know 5 is cutting into the middle lane, but X5 guards the basket area and covers 4 cutting deep.

Diagram 2-13 is put here to show you how easy it is to make a defensive adjustment ("36" to "35") without any changes on defensive coverage, but the offense must use a different attack to be successful.

The defense knows the call is "35"; therefore there will be a new habit pass to cover (Diagram 2-13). Under "35" coverage, both X2 and X3 play well off their assignment, helping X1 keep 1 from driving downcourt. When 1 sees this coverage, 1 knows he

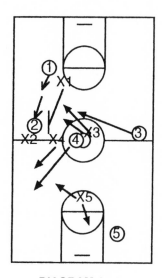

DIAGRAM 2-13

cannot drive between the defenders. 1 usually throws the pass to the uncovered 2. X2 now keeps 2 from driving downcourt as X1 races to set the trap with X2. Both trappers get against 2, encouraging 2 to begin his dribble. X2 and X1 ready themselves for the flick. 4 has cut diagonally to become the new habit pass receiver. But that is into the teeth of X4's coverage rule. X4 covers the strongside and the middle lane. (To see how to read coverage, study the section on interceptor's drills later in this chapter.) X3 covers the middle lane and the weakside lane. X5 cheats upcourt as the trap is set. Without other movement, the attack is doomed. Another offensive attack must be used or the defense wins.

You can scout your opponents and preplan how to take the offense out of any of its options. This will be discussed further in the sections in Chapter 7 on how to prepare a game plan and how to make adjustments during the game.

Let's say you have scouted your opponent and you know the passer will always become a cutter to the strongside lane (Diagram 2-14). 1 passes to 2 and cuts through as X2 and X1 set the trap ("35" is the call). The coverage does not change. In fact, 1 cuts into the teeth of X4's coverage. X4 must make sure he is on the ballside of 1's cut. X4 now covers the strongside lane, 1, and

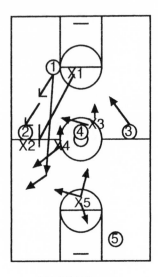

DIAGRAM 2-14

the middle lane, 4, shading the direction of 2's intentions. (See "Interceptor's Drills.") X3 covers the middle lane, 4, and the weakside lane, 3. X5 cheats upcourt as the trap is set.

The habit pass is always the first covered—it is the most immediate and most dangerous. The two immediate passing lanes are covered next. The weakside lane is the farthest away, and it takes a great passer to pass-cross his body to this lane (keep in mind that the dribbler is headed toward the strongside lane). The safety can often pick off this weakside pass unless the dribbler picks up his dribble and pivots to pass toward the weakside. But if the dribbler does this, the interceptors are reading the dribbler's eyes and motions, and they adjust by sliding back to those lanes. Both interceptors in the umbrella really have two lanes to cover, and they slide, reading the passer's intentions. (More on this in the "Interceptor's Drills" section.)

Safety or All-Out

Now you must decide when you want to go ALL OUT instead of staying in the SAFETY mode. We encourage this all-out mode once every ten possessions. The all-out mode changes only the safety's responsibility. In the all-out mode the safety cheats even further up the court and fills the weakside lane. Now there is a trap on the ballhandler and there is man-to-man coverage on the first attacker in each of the lanes. The only player left open is the one farthest down the court. But this man is covered in all cases except the all-out mode. The attacker with the ball has not been used to passing all the way downcourt, so he will not even consider this option. A turnover usually results in the all-out mode when not used too often.

Interceptor's Drills

Two drills are used to teach the interceptor's part of the defense. The first is called the Triangle Deflection Drill, and its primary purpose is to teach the interceptors to read the eyes and body motion of the passer. The second is called the Game Interceptor's Drill, and its primary purpose it to teach the coverage rules. Also, from this Game Interceptor's Drill the interceptors and trappers are taught how to recover from successful passes out of the traps.

TRIANGLE DEFLECTION DRILL

(Diagram 2-15)

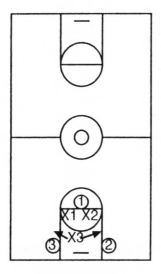

DIAGRAM 2-15

Objectives:

1. To teach trapping.
2. To teach the step-through.
3. To teach flicking from behind on dribblers who split traps.
4. To teach interceptors how to read the intentions of the passer.
5. To teach interceptors to intercept passes.
6. To teach trappers to keep their hands in the plane of the ball.

Procedure:

1. Put three attackers against three defenders.
2. 1 starts with the ball. He may pass to either 2 or 3.
3. 1 may step through and dribble. So may 2 or 3 when he gets the ball.
4. X1 and X2 trap 1, keeping their bodies against 1 and keeping their hands in the plane of the ball.
5. X3 splits 2 and 3, reading 1's intentions and body motion. X3 gets in motion toward the intended pass.
6. If 1 successfully gets the ball to 2, X3 and X2 trap 2. X1 now splits 1 and 3, reading 2's intentions.
7. If 1 successfully gets the ball to 3, X3 and X1 trap 3. X2 now reads 3's intentions while splitting 1 and 2.
8. The drill continues until the defense gets three deflections or interceptions. Then the offense becomes the defense, and three more players move to offense.
9. As the season progresses you may separate the attackers with greater distance. It is best to begin the season with 1 inside the free-throw circle and 2 and 3 on the big blocks.

GAME INTERCEPTOR'S DRILL

(Diagram 2-16)

This drill is used not only to teach interceptors their coverage rules but also to teach recovery out of successful passes out of traps (see the next section). You may start this drill

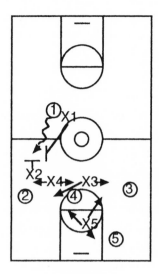

DIAGRAM 2-16

anywhere on the court. We are showing the drill from the twenty area. It is best to begin teaching it at the twenty area then expanding it downcourt. As the season progresses it is best to use the drill where you intend to use your press most in the next game.

Objectives:

1. To teach trapping techniques.
2. To teach interceptors to read the eyes and body motion of the passer.
3. To teach the coverage rules of the interceptors.
4. To teach recovery out of successful passes out of traps.
5. To teach defenders how to recognize the different calls and be in proper position to execute them.

Procedure:

1. Line up players in offensive attack formation (in Diagram 2-16, players are in 1-3-1 formation).
2. Coach makes a defensive call and defenders respond (in Diagram 2-16, the call is "26").

3. The "26" call is a trap on the dribbler, so X2 keeps 2 from getting the pass and races to trap 1 as 1 crosses the midcourt line. X1 stays to trap.

4. X4 covers the strongside lane and the middle lane.

5. X3 covers the weakside lane and the middle lane.

6. X5 covers the basket area unless an all-out mode has been called.

7. Each of the interceptors reads 1's intentions, moving as 1 adjusts his position.

8. X1 and X2 keep their hands in the plane of the ball, adjusting their hands as 1 adjusts the ball position.

9. After an interception or completion (defenders rotate to recovery positions; see the next section), the coach gathers the defense and makes another call. After players learn the coverage rules, this drill should be run at the area of the next game plan.

USED

During the course of the game, dribblers will often pick up their dribble with no teammate open to receive a pass. When you activate the run and jumps ("2" or "3"), the dribbler will sometimes pick up the dribble. When this happens, "Used" is immediately commenced. If this occurs in the back court, the opponents have ten seconds to get the ball over half-court. If this develops in the front court, the opponents must pass the ball within five seconds or a violation is called.

A full-court five-on-five drill is used to teach Used. No dribble is allowed. Therefore every defender overplays his assignment over the entire court. When an offensive player receives a pass, he must find a teammate open. He cannot dribble.

Used is always part of the defense whenever an attacker picks up his dribble and there has been no double-team—for example, excessive pressure when "40," "30," or "20" is run. Another great example: In all run-and-jump situations, after seeing a trap in a previous possession, the dribbler will frequently pick up his dribble. Used is immediately the cry of the defense.

RECOVERY

There are four coaching points (teaching points) that remain constant regardless of the tactic called or the area from which it was called. There are three passes from which recovery must take place and one constant about who leaves the trap. The habit pass is always covered by the defender who began in the center lane. A pass to the other lane will be covered by the original weakside defender. Any deep penetrating pass will be covered by the original safety. While these passes out of the trap are being covered by the above defenders, the other defenders race to the basket area to regroup. The runner (defender who goes to help trap) always recovers to find the open attacker.

Diagrams 2-17 through 2-19 show the three recovery techniques discussed above. Each of these diagrams is a continuation of Diagram 2-16, which was used to teach the Game Interceptor's Drill. As you recall, "26" was the call. Each of the three successful passing areas is discussed separately.

Diagram 2-17 displays the successful pass into the strongside lane. X1 and X2 trapped 1. X4 covers the strongside lane and the middle lane, and X3 covers the middle lane and the weakside lane.

DIAGRAM 2-17

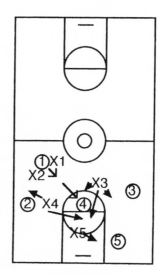

DIAGRAM 2-18

X5 is the safety. While the pass is on its way toward 2, all defenders except X4 race toward the basket area. Upon completion of the pass, X4 takes 2. X4 also calls out the number of his assignment, #4 in Diagrams 2-16 and 2-17. This call of #4 cues X2, the runner, whom he is to cover. All the other defenders take their original assignment: X1 stays with 1, X5 takes 5, and X3 blankets 3.

Diagram 2-18 is used to show recovery coverage should the pass be completed into other lanes. If the pass is completed to 3, X3 would cover 3 if 3 is in a high weakside lane. All defenders would then recover to their own assignments.

Diagram 2-18 shows a pass from 1 into the center lane to 4. X4 or X3 could have coverage (per coverage rule) on this successful pass. The defender in the best position should cover this new receiver. If it is X4, then all defenders would pick up their original assignments. If it is X3, then X3 calls out #3 to let X2, the runner, know his new assignment is 3. X4 would have 2, the attacker in the strongside lane. X1 stays with 1, X3 has 4, and X2 recovers on 3.

Diagram 2-19 illustrates a recovery pattern when the pass is successfully made to a weakside attacker far downcourt. If the pass

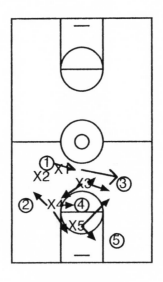

DIAGRAM 2-19

is made far downcourt, X5 is within his coverage rule to gamble for this interception. Should X5 arrive late, he must close out the new pass receiver. As X5 picks up 3, X5 is yelling #5 to let X2 know who his new assignment is. X4 takes 2, the attacker in the strongside lane. X3 takes the attacker in the middle lane, 4; and X1 stays with 1. It would take two successful passes to get the layup from the twenty area positioning shown in Diagram 2-19. X2 can often recover and steal this second pass. X2 can always recover to a position not to allow this second pass to be made.

Unfortunately every pass is not stolen or deflected. Many are completed, so a recovery strategy must be developed to prevent further penetration of the basketball. Our recovery strategy is simple:

1. The defender who was the runner on the trap recovers on the open man.
2. There are three successful passing areas:
    a. The pass to the strongside lane is covered by the original center-lane defender.
    b. The pass to the center lane or the weakside lane (the other lane) is covered by the original weakside defender.
    c. And if the pass is far downcourt (you can even pick distances; for example, if the trap is in the thirty area, a pass to the ten area would represent a pass far downcourt), the safety picks up the new pass receiver.

Proper recovery is essential to a great press. Just because the attacking team manages to pass out of a trap, it should not follow that the attacking team scores. In fact, if proper defensive recovery is accomplished, the press can be run all night without allowing a layup.

Proper recovery is drilled nightly using the Game Interceptor's Drill. This drill should be run from the area you intend to use most in your next game plan, using the tactic you plan to use most. After a full season of drilling, it is easy to see how the press is especially effective at the most important time of the year: Tournament Time.

STRATEGIES DEVELOPED

There are four divisions where you want to develop your strategy: You have to pick the court markers; you have to pick the tactic you want to use at that court marker; you have to pick the attacker you want to use that tactic on; and you want to pick the weakest area in the opponent's team attack. Several different ideas are offered here to help you determine each division of your strategy.

Picking the Court Marker

1. Offensive teams that are quicker than the defensive team should be defended at the smaller court area, namely the twenties and the tens and inside the ten.
2. Conversely, offensive teams that are slower than defensive teams should be pressed at the forty or thirty level.
3. Teams with poor patterns (less than three outlet pass areas) should be pressed at the court marker of those poor patterns.
4. Teams that get the ball in slowly should face the 40 presses.
5. Teams that get the ball in quickly but do not handle the ball well should experience the 30 presses.
6. Generally speaking, taller teams should be defended in the forty and thirty areas.

Picking the Tactic

1. Great point guards should be played at the forty and thirty levels, denied the ball, and trapped if they get it back, and then denied again.
2. Great post players should be trapped inside the ten area.
3. Weak-shooting perimeter players should see their defender being used to help trap other stronger offensive players.

4. A big forward type who has a good one- or two-step dribble to the basket should see "35" or "45." This would require a further dribble attack than a dribble or two.

5. Players who can be stressed mentally by a press should be pressured using a variety of tactics (run and jump, trapped at different areas using different traps, hedged, etc.).

6. Teams that are highly patterned should be trapped often and with a variety of traps.

7. Teams that move slowly up the court should face traps.

8. Teams that clear out should face "49."

9. Teams that move quickly and pass well should see "44," "34," "40," and "30."

10. Coaches who hate being trapped usually instill this fear subconsciously into their ball clubs. These teams should see the "5's," the "6's," and the "7's" from all areas of the court.

11. Take the dribblers out of their game by running the "5's."

12. Take the passers out of their game by running the "0's."

13. Teams with poor ballhandling big men should face the "49" call often, with the defenders on the big poor ballhandler going to help trap the ballhandling guard.

Picking the Players

1. Poor dribblers or awkward players, such as tall uncoordinated players, should be trapped off the pass, bumped against, and compelled to split the trap with a dribble.

2. Great-scoring big men should face "9" calls, using the defender on the weakest outside shooter as the helper on the trap.

3. Weaker physical players should be compelled to receive the pass, then be bumped and pressed, the "5's."

4. Players with poor peripheral vision should be pressed both off the dribble and receiving the pass.

5. Players who pick up their dribble prematurely should be trapped or run and jumped.

6. Smaller players should be trapped often. They cannot see over the defenders, much less pass to an open teammate.

7. Basically great players should be denied the ball, trapped when they get it, then denied the ball again. They will soon tire of this constant pressure.

8. Basically weaker players should be trapped constantly. The defenders on these weaker players can also be used to trap the stronger players.

How to Study Patterns As an Aid

1. Cutters who pass and cut should be jammed. This is best done in a smaller area, like the twenties or tens, or inside the ten.

2. Teams without three passing lanes in their patterns should be pressed in the area where those three passing lanes do not exist.

3. Teams without three passing lanes off a pass should be allowed to receive the pass in that area, then trapped there.

4. Teams without three passing lanes off a dribble should see the "6's" and the "7's" all night.

5. Teams that do not attack the basket but are content to get the ball into the front court then set up their half-court offense should see the "40's" and the "30's." You have everything to gain and nothing to lose against such a ball club.

These by no means represent all the different considerations you can take in deciding where to press, who to press, what to use as your press, and what to attack in the other team's offensive system. But this gives you a good idea of how to go about making these decisions.

The next five chapters present all ten tactics from each of the five areas. Each of the ten tactics has explanations of the coverage rule being applied and of proper recovery from successful passes. Each tactic also has a section on the reasons why you want to run that tactic in that area. After reading those reasons coupled with the above section, you should be able to devise your own game plan and make it work with proper bench decisions.

Chapter *3*

How to Teach the 40 Series

You should read and reread the first two chapters, making sure you understand the teaching of the tactic, the coverage rules, the recovery rules, and when it is best to run a particular call. This will enable you to better understand the presentation of each type of tactic. You can decide on a game plan and use the illustrations in Chapters 3 through 7 as drills to teach your players the proper basics.

All the fundamentals, the basics, the tactics, the strategies, and the calls were presented in the first two chapters. Now it is time to show how these rudiments actually work during a ball game. Of course all situations cannot be presented; space does not permit it. But samples from all calls are shown, starting with "0" calls through the "9" calls. This chapter presents the 40 series, that is, "40" through "49." Each section presents the coverage rule as well as recovery out of any successful pass and the best times to run that particular call.

"40"

By the rules, the "40" press begins at the forty area, the end-bounds line. The "0" tells the defenders it is the regular defense, meaning individual coverage with complete denial of any down-court pass. All passes are downcourt, because the ball begins out of bounds.

It is best to run "40" at the beginning of the game. It gets the defense in the proper frame of mind with pressure, and yet all attackers are covered. Also, you can pick up the intended attack of the opposition. You can analyze this attack to find where the opposition will not have three passing lanes, then store this knowledge for later defensive calls.

"41"

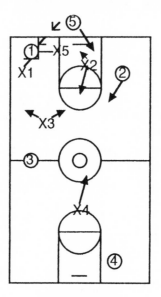

DIAGRAM 3-1

"1" calls ask for a trap on first ball movement. This means when the ball is inbounded by 5, X5 will go trap with the defender on the ball receiver (in Diagram 3-1, X5 will trap with X1). This gives the look of a 1-2-1-1 zone press.

As the ball comes into 1, X1 and X5 trap. X2 covers both 2 and 5 per the coverage rules. X3 covers the downcourt lane (3 in Diagram 3-1). When the trap is set, X4 comes up near midcourt to help in the passing lanes. There is no middle-lane attacker, so the weakside defender, X2, covers the middle lane and the weakside lane. X3 covers the strongside lane and the weakside lane. X3 covers the strongside lane and helps out in the middle lane. X4 plays safety and helps with middle-lane coverage.

To recover out of successful passes the recovery rule is used. A pass to either 5 or 2 would be covered by X2. X5, the runner (see Chapter 2) would race to cover the open man, the attacker not covered by X2. X1 stays with 1, X3 picks up 3, and X4 covers 4.

A pass to 3 would find X3 covering 3 and all defenders picking their assignments back up. The same is true for a successful pass downcourt to 4. X4 would cover 4 while all defenders picked up their own assignments.

The "41" call works best after a few "40" calls, and the opposition attacks by clearing out. The quick trap immediately puts the opposition into a defensive frame of mind, setting up later steals, beginning to build confusion. "41" works extremely well when the opposition's point guard is smaller than the two trappers (X1 and X5 in Diagram 3-1).

"42"

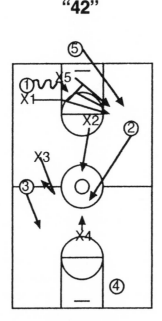

DIAGRAM 3-2

After a few "40" calls followed by a few "41" calls, "42" becomes a very effective tool. 1 has the ball (Diagram 3-2) while his teammates begin to clear out. X1 compels 1 to dribble to the middle. X5 immediately activates the two-man run and jump ("2" tactics: see Chapter 1). X5 picks up 1 and X1 goes to cover 5.

There are no coverage rules because the defense is not a trap, and there are no recovery rules because no one is left open. X5 and X1 merely exchange men. "42" is designed to help cause confusion for calls later in the game.

"42" is best used after a few traps. 1 in Diagram 3-2 cannot determine if X5's movements represent a trap or a run and jump; consequently, 1 often will pick up his dribble. If 1 does pick up his dribble, then the entire defense is in man-to-man coverage and the dribble Used drill is activated.

"43"

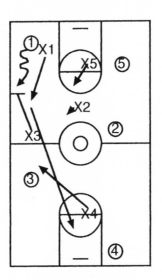

DIAGRAM 3-3

All "3" tactics are three-man run and jumps. In Diagram 3-3, 1 is forced up the outside lane by X1. X3 activates the three-man run and jump with X4 covering the outside lane and X1 leaving 1 to pick up the open attacker, 4. X5 and X2 keep coverage on their assignments.

While the two-man run and jump is shown with action toward the middle lane and the three-man run and jump is shown with action down the outside lane, it does not follow that all two-man run and jumps go inside and all three-man run and jumps go outside. Both can go in either direction.

The coverage rule does not come into play because there is no trap. The recovery rule is simple: If a pass is completed to 3, X4 would pick up 3, X1 would pick up 4, and X3 would stay with 1.

"43," like "42," is best run after a few traps have been set. The dribbler, 1 in Diagram 3-3, cannot tell if the defense intends to trap or to run and jump. Should 1 pick up his dribble, all defenders have one-on-one assignments, impelling the dribble Used phase of the "0" defense.

"44"

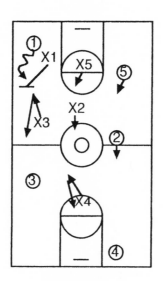

DIAGRAM 3-4

"44" is explained by expanding Diagram 3-3 into Diagram 3-4. This will show how changing from "43" to "44" changes passing possibilities. 1 has the ball in Diagram 3-4. 5 has moved inbounds. X1 impels 1 to begin his dribble down the side lane. X3 activates the hedge and recovers by racing hard toward 1, then retreating quickly. 1 will hesitate to pass to the open 3 until he can see if any defender is racing to cover that lane. This hesitation by 1 allows X3 time to recover. If 1 changes direction and begins to dribble toward 5, X5 will race hard toward 1, showing the hedge and recover. 1 will probably advance the ball slowly down the floor.

There is no coverage rule because there is no trap. There is no recovery rule because no defender will leave his assignment.

"44" is best run after a few traps. It is even more effective when there have been traps in other areas, like the twenty or the thirty area. When traps have been set in the thirty area, for example, it leaves 1 unsure if X3's or X5's movement is the beginning of a trap.

"44" coupled with "36" (or "37") is an extremely effective combination (see Chapter 7). It is easy to see how "44" permits 1 to dribble slowly downcourt. This slow dribble takes time off the ten-second count. Then as 1 crosses the thirty marker, the defender assigned to go set the trap activates the thirty call (either "36" or "37"). Because the ten-second count is elapsing, the attacker hurries into a mistake, hopefully leading to an interception and an easy basket. X1 can make this phase of the press even more effective by pressuring 1 using the zigzag drill technique.

"45"

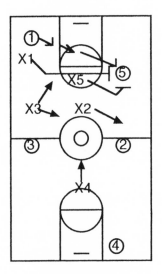

DIAGRAM 3-5

It is sometimes beneficial to draw a line just inside the full-court marker and call it the forty area. We do that so we can run a "45" that is different from "41." "41" names a trap with the first ball movement, and "45" calls trapping the first pass receiver after the ball is advanced beyond the named court marker. The drawing of "45" shows the movement after the ball has been inbounded (much like Diagram 3-2).

Both X3 and X5 sag toward the ball, inviting the pass to one of their assignments, 3 and 5 respectively. In Diagram 3-5 the pass goes to 5. X1 races to help X5 trap 5. X2, per the coverage rule, covers the strongside wing and the center lane while X3 defends the middle lane and the pass to 1 or 3. X4, once the trap is set, can come as far as midcourt to help.

Should 5 successfully pass out of the trap to 1, X3 would take 1. X1 would recover onto 3 unless X4 had come to cover 3. In the latter case, X1 would rotate all the way back to 4. X5 keeps 5 and X2 blankets 2. A pass by 5 to 2 would have X2 cover 2 and all players keep their assignments. Also, a pass by 5 to 4 or to 3 requires all players to keep their assignments.

A great time to run "45" would occur, of course, if 5 is a poor ballhandler and this is your opponent's press offense. Also, when teams advance the ball by a few dribbles, then pass, then a few dribbles, then pass, this trap works wonders. When a team has a great point guard who likes to dribble-penetrate, the "5' tactics work extremely well because of the exaggerated help from nearby defensive teammates.

"46"

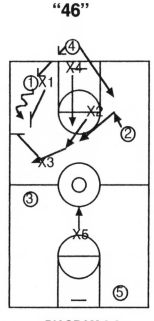

DIAGRAM 3-6

A "6" call names trapping the dribbler from straight on. "46" represents this at the full-court level. The pass has been inbounded to 1. The adjustment line is anywhere inside the 40 to 30 markers. This tactic begins to look just like the 2-2-1 zone press. As 1 begins this dribble downcourt, X1 will not allow 1 to change direction (Diagram 3-6). X3, the defender in the strongside lane, races to help X1 trap 1. X2, per the coverage rule when there is no middle-lane defender, must hustle to cover the habit pass (the strongside lane). X2 also helps in the middle lane. X4 drops quickly into the middle lane, his primary responsibility, and X4 shades the pass back to 4. Once the trap is set, X5 can come up near midcourt.

The recovery rule requires X4 to pick up 4 if 1 passes out of the trap to 4. X3 would race over to cover 2 unless X5 has come to cover 2, then X3 would go to cover 5. X2 would guard 3 while X1 picks up his own assignment. A completed pass to 3 would see X2 covering 3, X3 defending 2, and the other three guarding their assignments. A completed pass to 5 would require all defenders to guard their assignments.

"6" tactics are effective against great ballhandling point guards. They are far away from where they can do damage, and they are constantly being double-teamed. This strategy also works well after a few run and jumps or hedge and recoveries.

"47"

A "7" tactic calls trapping the dribbler from the weakside. This makes it mandatory for X1 to compel 1 to change his direction. X1 must hustle to accomplish this. Just as 1 reverse dribbles, X4 races to help X1 put on the trap (Diagram 3-7). X2 covers the habit pass and the center lane. X3 covers what is now the weakside lane; 3 is the player in the weakside lane and the middle lane. X5 races upcourt to the midcourt line once the trap is set, unless the all-out trap is called. In case of the all-out trap, X5 would have the middle lane, X3 the new weakside lane, and X2 the new strongside lane.

A successful pass from 1 to 4, under the safety recovery rules, would see X2 picking up 4, and X1 rotating over to take 2 should

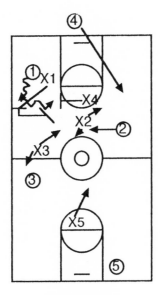

DIAGRAM 3-7

X5 not pick up 2. X4 would have 1 and X3 stay with 3. X5 ordinarily stays with 5.

This tactic is especially successful after running the "6" tactic a few possessions. It also works well against players who do not reverse dribble well. Many times these players pick up their dribble immediately instead of trying to fight the double-team.

"48"

The "8" calls deny a designated ballhandler the ball (1 in the case of Diagram 3-8). Should this designated ballhandler get the ball back, a double-team immediately occurs.

X4, the defender on the inbounds passer, double-teams 1. X1 gets behind 1. X2 does not deny 2 the ball. 4 usually will pass inbounds to 2 because it is the line of least resistance (Diagram 3-8). Once 2 has the ball, X4 goes back to 4, and the team runs the "0" call unless 1 fights X1 to get open. When 1 receives a pass, the double-team occurs. X4 and X1 would double-team 1. X2 would take the middle lane and the right lane while X3 takes the middle

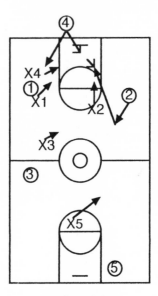

DIAGRAM 3-8

lane and the left lane. X5 plays safety. Should 1 want to attack the double-team with the dribble, X4 and X1 stay with 1, and X2 and X3 adjust their positioning. Once 1 passes, the "0" tactic is run. This continues until 1 gets out of the habit of going to get the pass back.

Recovery is simple. Everyone usually hustles back to their assignments. But should a pass to 4 be successful and 4 begins a dribble drive toward front court (we usually know who throws the ball in and how successful they will be in dribble penetration), another defender might have to stop the advancement of the ball. Whichever defender stops this advancement calls out his assignment. The defender on 4, X4, would hustle to take his teammate's assignment. For example, if X2 stopped 4, then X4 would pick up 2.

It is best to run this tactic when 2 is not a very good dribbling guard. Most teams have a great shooting guard at this position. That same shooting guard usually is not a great dribble penetrant. Also, it helps when the attacker throwing the ball is a big man who does not bring the ball down the floor with skill. Using the "8" tactic the defense can completely disrupt the opponent's offensive scheme, and this tactic can often take a great point guard completely out of the game.

"49"

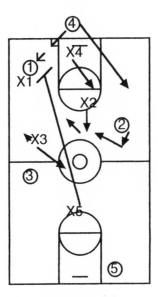

DIAGRAM 3-9

Do not run the "9" calls often or offenses will zero in on this tactic and score easy layups. "9" calls name trapping with a designated trapper. In the case of Diagram 3-9, the designated trapper is the post defender, X5 (by rule, it does not have to be the post defender). X5 races upcourt when the ball is entered into the court by 4. Now we have an all-out trap called. X5 and X1 double-team 1. 1 is so much smaller than the post defender that it will be almost impossible for 1 to look over the double-team and find 5 unless 1 is looking for it. X4 guards 4, X2 guards 2, and X3 defends 3. There is a double-team and no open immediate attacker.

No recovery is necessary. All defenders must deny their assignment the ball. If 1 successfully passes out of the trap, then all defenders must race hard to the basket area to prevent the layup. Once the defenders are near their basket, the defenders can again pick up their assignments.

It is best to run this attack after several "8" calls. 1, in that case, suspects the open attacker to be near him in the back court. This usually gets a turnover.

In this chapter I have shown how the tactics work from the forty area. Each section discussed the coverage rule and how it applied. Each section also covered the recovery rule from any successful pass out of the trap and the best times to run the tactic.

In other words the coverage and recovery rules of Chapter 2 and the tactics of Chapter 1 were followed in each instance. Roughly, you want to run the 40 series anytime you have a quicker ball club than your opponents. If the opposition has one or two quicker people, you can take those quicker players out of the game with "8" and "9" calls. Use your quickness to your advantage. The next chapter presents the tactics from the thirty area: same fundamentals, same calls, same coverage rules, same recovery rules—but a whole new set of problems for the opposition. That is one of the great advantages of the adjustable area press: nothing new to teach the defense, but the offense must have a completely new set of attack principles. It's hard for the attackers to learn a whole new set of attack principles and still practice their half-court attack.

Chapter 4

How to Teach the 30 Series

The 40 series was explained in Chapter 3; the 30 series is clarified in Chapter 4. In Chapter 3, all tactics from "0" through "9" were presented with an open middle lane; but in Chapter 4, all tactics from "0" through "9" are displayed with a post player in the middle lane. This permits more discussion on the coverage rule with a middle-lane player. It also allows for better understanding of the recovery process (following the recovery rules) because now defenders must adjust to cover the middle-lane attackers. Most full-court and three-quarter-court press offenses use a middle-lane attacker.

Each section presents a diagram for review. Coverage rules govern who covers what lane, and the applicable coverage rules are noted in each section. Passes out of traps allow for discussion of the recovery rules. And the best times to run each particular call also receive treatment.

"30"

The "0" means the press is in its regular denial of any downcourt passes. The "3" tells the defense to pick up at the thirty level, the imaginary line just above the free-throw circle. So "30" tells the defense to pick up their assignments at the thirty marker and deny all downcourt passes, using help-and-recover techniques.

There are no traps, so there is no need for the coverage or the recovery rules. Every defender keeps his own assignment.

Thirty is run instead of forty when the opposition gets the ball in quickly preventing immediate denial defense after a made basket. Picking up at the thirty level prevents the attackers from getting their fast break after made baskets. It also allows the defense to activate the "0" part of the press.

Thirty is best run at the beginning of the game against teams who enter the pass quickly. It allows the defensive coach to study the press attack of the opposition. By studying the planned attack, the defensive coach can make adjustments later in the game.

"31"

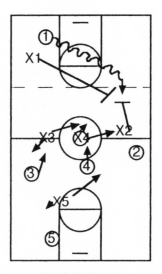

DIAGRAM 4-1

In Diagram 4-1, the designated trapper with the first ball movement is X2. You have determined from scouting reports that 2, a shooting guard, does not penetrate with the ball extremely well. So X2 goes to trap 1 (Diagram 4-1). X1 helps X2 trap. By the coverage rule, X4 would cover the habit pass (the strongside lane) and the middle lane. X3 covers the middle lane and the weakside lane. If 1 keeps his dribble live, then X1 and X2 continue to trap while the defenders in the passing lanes adjust.

If 1 passes to 2, X4 would recover on 2. X3 would cover 4, and X2 would pick up 3. X1 and X5 would maintain coverage on their assignments. If 1 passes to 4, X3 would cover 4. X2 would have to hurry to regain coverage on 3, and X4 would keep 2. X1 and X5 again keep their assignments. A completed pass out of the trap to either 3 or 5 would have each defender recovering onto their original assignments.

When the "1" tactic is used, it is always best to pick the defender of the attacker who does not drive well to the basket to be a designated trapper. This means a completed pass out of the trap will not hurt the defense. Running "31" after a few run and jumps might even cause 1 to pick up his dribble when he sees the trap.

"32"

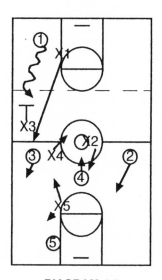

DIAGRAM 4-2

"2" calls activate two-man run and jumps. Diagram 4-2 displays the two-man run and jump to the outside lane. X1 guides 1 down the outside lane, and X3 keeps his body between 3 and 1. As 1 crosses the thirty-area line, X3 races toward 1. X3 and X1 exchange assignments. All other defenders deny their assignments the pass.

There is no trap, so there is no need for the coverage or the recovery rules. Each defender keeps his own assignment, except for X1 and X3 who exchange assignments.

Running "2" calls after a few traps frequently impels the dribbler, 1 in Diagram 4-2, to pick up the dribble. When this happens, it activates the Used drill of the "0" tactic.

"33"

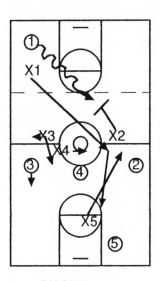

DIAGRAM 4-3

"3" tactics compel the three-man run and jump. This time the three-man run and jump occurs toward the middle of the court. As 1 dribbles across the thirty marker, X2 races to activate the run and jump (Diagram 4-3). Just as X2 leaves, X5 leaves to cover the habit pass. X3 can drop to help on coverage on 5. X1 leaves and races hard to cover 5. X3 and X4 keep their assignments.

There is no trap; hence, there is no need for the coverage or the recovery rules. X3 can, if 1 has a tendency to throw deep, initially help on coverage on 5. But proper pressure by X1 should prevent 1 from finding this opening.

Three-man run and jumps work best after a few traps have

been set ("6" or "7" calls). This prior trapping has a tendency to compel 1 into picking up his dribble. Used is always activated when a dribbler picks up his dribble, and each defender has responsibility for his own assignment (or, as is the case in run and jumps, responsibility for a designated assignment).

"34"

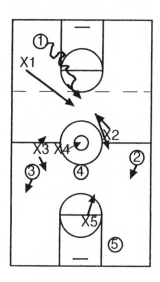

DIAGRAM 4-4

"4" tactics name hedge-and-recover maneuvers. As 1 crosses the thirty marker with his dribble, X2 races hard a few steps toward 1. X2 keeps his body between 2 and 1, discouraging the pass from 1. X2 immediately recovers onto 2. X4 and X5 might even cheat toward 2 in case 1 passes to 2. A pass from 1 would have to be one of the two slower passes: the lob or the bounce pass. Hopefully, 1 will pick up his dribble as X2 recovers onto 2. This activates the Used part of the "0" tactic. This often happens.

There is no trap, so there is no need for the coverage or the recovery rules. Each defender keeps his own assignment.

Hedge and recoveries work best after a few traps. 1, in Diagram 4-4, does not know if a trap is about to occur when X2 races toward him, so 1 might pick up his dribble. Once X2 recovers onto 2, 1 would have no place to pass the ball. Hedge and recoveries slow down the pace of the ball game, and "4" calls often confuse the ballhandler when the next trap occurs.

"35"

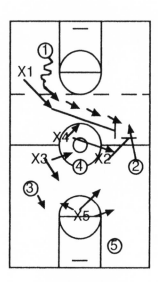

DIAGRAM 4-5

"5" tactics name a trap on the first pass after the ball crosses the named marker. As 1 dribbles across the thirty marker, both X2 and X3 have sagged toward the inside lane, preventing 1 from continuing his dribble even if he beats X1. The line of least resistance is to pass to 2 (Diagram 4-5).

Regardless of where 2 receives the pass, X2 and X1 will trap 2. Because there is a center-lane attacker, X4 mentally moves to cover the habit pass (the strongside lane) and the middle lane. But X4 does not want to guard space. If no attacker exists in the strongside lane, X4 would shade the middle lane. X3, the weakside defender, shifts to cover the middle lane and to shade the weakside lane. X5, upon the trap, comes up the court to help on any errant pass.

A completed pass back to 1 finds X3 covering 1. X4 takes the post player 4, X1 rotates to cover 3. X5 plays his assignment. A completed pass to 4 finds X3 covering 4, X4 rotating to 3, X5 on 5, X1 on 1, and X2 on 2. A completed pass crosscourt to 3 would find all defenders picking up their original assignments.

"35" should be used actively against great point guards. The sag by the wings discourages the dribble by 1, and "5" calls put the ball into less capable ballhandlers, possibly creating a turnover. "5" calls combined with "4" calls can really be confusing to the dribbler. When run and jumps are added ("2" and "3" calls), turnovers often result.

"36"

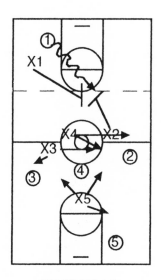

DIAGRAM 4-6

"6" means a trap from straight on. X1, in Diagram 4-6, compels 1 to dribble toward the right sideline. X1 must not let 1 reverse direction. As 1 crosses the thirty maker, X2 races to set the trap with X1. X2 stays between 2 and 1. X4, per the coverage rule, covers the habit passing lane (the strongside lane) and shades the middle lane. X3 rotates to the middle lane and shades the weakside lane. Upon seeing the trap set, X5 can come upcourt some to help intercept any slow errant pass.

The recovery rule compels X4 to take 2 if 1 successfully finds 2. X3 would take 4 and X2 would rotate to cover 3. X1 and X5 keep their assignments. A successful pass to 4 finds X3 covering 4, X4 on 2, X2 racing to cover 3, and X1 and X5 again keeping their assignments. A completed pass to either 3 or 5 requires all defenders to pick up their original assignments.

"6" calls work wonders against poor ballhandling guards. "36" coupled with almost any non-trapping 40 series often results in ten-second violations. Aggressive, quick teams would want to run the traps ("5," "6," and "7") alternately in all areas for the entire duration of the game.

"37"

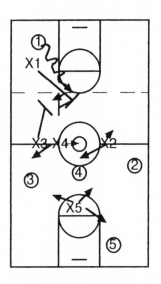

DIAGRAM 4-7

"7" tactics impel trapping the ballhandler from the weakside. This trap should occur just as the dribbler reverses his direction. 1, in Diagram 4-7, dribbles toward the right sideline. X1 forces a change in direction just as 1 crosses the thirty marker. All defenders know this, cheating toward the commencement of the "37" call. Just as 1 changes direction (Diagram 4-7), X3 races to help X1 trap. X4 moves toward the habit pass (the left-side lane) and shades the middle lane. X2 slides toward the middle lane but shades the weakside lane. X5, upon seeing the trap set, comes up the court to help on weakly thrown passes.

To recover on a pass to 3, X4 would take 3, X2 would cover 4, and X3 would blanket 2. X1 and X5 would keep their assignments. On the all-out press, X5 would come up and take the weakside lane but shade the deep coverage. All-out traps should be run very sparingly (see Chapter 2). A successful pass to 4, under the safety press, would find X2 covering 4, X4 guarding 3, and X3 rotating to 2. Again, X1 and X5 would keep their assignments. A successful pass to 2 or 5 would result in all defenders guarding their own assignments.

"7" calls, like "6" calls, are very aggressive traps. They take good dribbling guards out of the attack, and they compel poor ballhandling guards into many turnovers. When "7" is run after a 40 call, such as a 40 run and jump, the dribbling attacker frequently hits the panic button (because of the ten-second count) and throws the ball away.

"38"

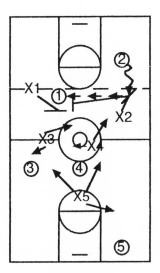

DIAGRAM 4-8

The "8" calls are designed to take an attacker out of the game. In the thirty and forty areas the attacker you want to take out of the game is the good dribbling guard, usually the point guard. Diagram 4-8 shows 1 being denied the inbounds pass, and 2 dribbling the ball up the court as 1 again gets himself open. When 1 gets open, 2 passes to 1 (Diagram 4-8). X2 immediately goes to trap 1. X4 covers the habit pass back to 2, and X4 shades the middle lane. Remember, you have made a decision before the game that 2 is not a dangerous driver to the basket. That is why you are trapping with X2. X3 guards the middle lane and shades the left outside lane. X5 comes up the court when he sees the good trap set.

A successful pass back to 2 rotates X4 to 2, X3 to 4, and X2 to 3. Another pass back to 1 would again activate "38," and this time X4 would be the trapper (the defender on 2). The other two defenders, X1 and X5, maintain coverage on their assignments. A pass to 4 finds X3 on 4, X4 on 2, and X2 on 3. X1 and X5 keep their assignments. A pass to 3 or to 5 results in all defenders keeping their assignments.

"38" is perfect to take a good dribbling guard out of the offensive full-court attack. Couple "38" with an occasional "39" and you can confuse even the best point guard.

"39"

When the opposition is known to clear out frequently, a "9" call will take them out of this attack. As 1 dribbles over the thirty marker, X5, who has cheated upcourt, races to help X1 trap 1. X2, X3, and X4 guard their assignments, with the weakside defender, X2 in Diagram 4-9, shading the deep attacker. This is really an all-out trap.

A successful pass to either 3 or 4 would find all defenders on their assignments, except X2 who covers 5 and X5 who covers 2. A successful pass to 2 results in X2 covering 2, X4 guarding 4, X5 taking 3, and X3 recovering to 5.

"39" is best run when the defense desperately needs a turnover and an ensuing layup basket. "9" tactics should be activated very seldom. A coach needs to pick and choose his times for this defensive attack.

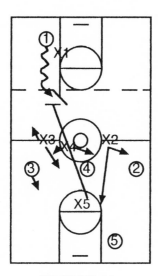

DIAGRAM 4-9

If you have read and reread the rudiments of Chapters 1 and 2 (the tactics, the coverage rules, the recovery rules), you have fully understood the diagrams of this chapter. These diagrams can be used as drills to teach your game plan.

Each section of Chapter 4, like Chapter 3, has covered the diagram, the tactic, the coverage, and the recovery as well as the best times to run the particular call.

Chapter 5 covers the pressure defense from the twenty area. Again, you will see full treatment of the tactic, the coverage, and the recovery.

Chapter 5

How to Teach the 20 Series

The 20 series begins at the half-court line, making it very easy for all defenders to see when to begin cheating in their coverage. This entire area is best used when the defenders are not exceptionally quick. Twenty calls can take an attacking team completely out of all their offensive maneuvers, rendering their practice sessions useless.

As in the previous two chapters, all defensive calls covered in this chapter have the tactic explained, the coverage rule activated, and the recovery rules enunciated. The best times to run each call are also discussed.

"20"

"40"–"20" is a perfect call to begin a ball game. You can see the intended attack at both the full-court and the half-court levels and then store this knowledge for future tactic calls.

"20" is the basic defense. There are no traps, so there is no need for either the coverage or the recovery rules. All defenders guard their assignments.

"21"

Sometimes a team has a great shooting guard or scoring forward, and you want to take this player out of the game. This is easily done by activating the "9" calls. But you noticed during

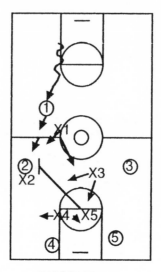

DIAGRAM 5-1

scouting that the opposition always enters their offense with a pass to the great wing player as the point guard dribbles over the half-court line. So you call "21." The opposition's center, 5, has weak hands and does not penetrate well off the dribble. So you designate X5 to trap with the first ball movement beyond half-court, the "21" call. 1 passes to 2 (Diagram 5-1). X5, who has cheated up the court, races to help X2 trap 2.

Because there is no middle-lane attacker, X4 covers the strongside lane and the middle lane. X3 guards the middle lane and shades the weakside lane. X1 defends the habit pass back to 1 and shades the middle lane. 2, the opposition's superstar, must defeat the double-team to be effective—a chore 2 is not going to be successful at the entire game long.

A pass by 2 to 1, 3, or 4 would have all players recovering to their own assignments. A successful pass to 5 would see X4 covering 5 while X5 would race hard to regain advantage on 4.

"1" calls can be used to take a perimeter player out of his half-court game. It also disrupts the precious timing of a smooth-running-machine type of offense. The "1" calls coupled with the "5" calls will completely take the superstar-wing type of player out of the game. And by mixing up these two calls, the wing player will have trouble finding his temporarily open teammate (a different habit passing lane is open in the "5" call than the one open in the "1" call).

"22"

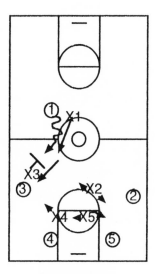

DIAGRAM 5-2

It is still safe to run and jump at the twenty level. "22" calls for the two-man run and jump. As 1 dribbles across the half-court line, X3 hustles to run and jump with X1. X4 can cheat toward 3 should 1 throw a soft pass to 3; otherwise, X1 and X3 merely switch assignments. X2 keeps 2, X4 stays with 4, and X5 defends 5.

There is no trap, so there is no need for either the coverage or the recovery rules. All defenders, except X1 and X3, keep their assignments.

Two-man run and jumps are used to confuse the good point guard. Those good dribblers never know when it is a trap instead of a run and jump. Many, when they see X3 racing toward them, will pick up their dribble. This activates the Used portion of the "0" defense.

"23"

"3" means a three-man run and jump. Diagram 5-3 displays this three-man run and jump. X3 runs toward 1 as 1 dribbles across the twenty marker (the half-court line). X4, because there is no center-lane attacker, comes from the baseline to jump in front of 3.

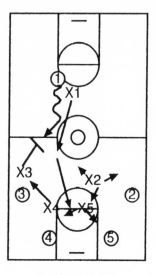

DIAGRAM 5-3

X4 leaves 4 just as X3 leaves 3. X1 rotates all the way back to 4. X5 helps to defend 4 until X1 arrives. X5 keeps 5, and X2 guards 2.

There is no trap, so there is no need for either the coverage or the recovery rules. The three men who run and jump exchange assignments, and the other two keep their original responsibilities.

It is safe to run and jump with three men at the twenty level, and the three-man run and jump can thoroughly confuse even the best point guard when coupled with the traps. Instead of just running the basic "20," "22" and "23" can be interwoven with the basic team defense.

"24"

"4" names a hedge and recovery. As 1 is dribbling up the court, X3 begins to cheat toward 1. X3 races toward 1 just as 1 crosses the half-court line. X4 cheats toward 3 to intercept the quick pass to 3 (Diagram-5-4). X3 keeps his body between 1 and 3. After a few steps, X3 retreats to his own assignment. This has the tendency to compel 1 to pick up his dribble especially if a few traps have already been run. When 1 picks up his dribble, the Used

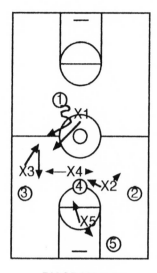

DIAGRAM 5-4

part of the basic defense is activated. Should 1 reverse his direction and dribble toward 2, X2 hedges toward 1 before recovering onto his own man, 2.

There is no trap, so there is no need for either the coverage or the recovery rules. All defenders keep their original assignments.

A hedge and recovery can be run at any time without giving up anything on defense. It is best run after a few traps have been called, especially the "6" and "7" calls. This has a tendency to impel 1 to pick up his dribble, starting the used portion of the "0" calls.

"25"

"5" names trapping the first pass receiver after the ball is advanced beyond the named court marker. As 1 crosses the half-court marker, X3 and X2 have sagged to help X1 stop the penetrating 1. When 1 sees 3 open, 1 will either pass to 3 or take on two defenders. The line of least resistance is to pass to 3. As 3 receives the pass, X3 and X1 trap (Diagram 5-5). X5 takes the strongside lane and shades the middle lane per the coverage rule.

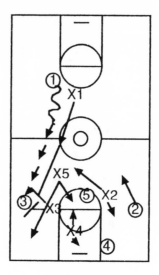

DIAGRAM 5-5

X2 takes the middle lane and the habit pass back to 1. X4 comes up a step or two to help on any slow errant pass.

A completed pass to 1 sees all defenders picking up their original assignments. A pass crosscourt to 2 would find X4 moving up to cover 2, X1 dropping hard to cover 4, X2 staying with 1, and X5 and X3 keeping their assignments. A pass to 5 would find all defenders keeping their assignments.

"25" is great for taking teams out of their often-used half-court attack. The opponents must have learned a different method of scoring than their ordinary man-to-man attack. "25" also limits the effectiveness of the point guard and can take a great scoring wing out of his game.

"26"

As 1 dribbles over the half-court line, X3 races to help X1 trap 1. X4 comes hard to cover the habit pass (the strongside lane). There is no middle-lane attacker so the strongside lane falls to X4, the next player down the court. X5 helps on 4 and also keeps his own assignment (Diagram 5-6). X2 shades to the middle lane and shades his own assignment.

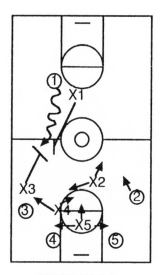

DIAGRAM 5-6

Should 3 receive a pass from 1, X4 would cover 3. X3 would race hard to cover either 4 or 5 (X5 would communicate this). X1 stays with 1, and X2 guards 2. A pass to 2 would find all defenders covering their own assignments. A completed pass to 4 would see X5 covering 4 and X2 covering 5. X4 would take 3, and X3 would guard 2.

To take a point guard out of the game, the "6" and the "7" traps should be utilized. Couple these two traps with the "8" and the "9" calls, and the point guard has been eliminated as an offensive source.

"27"

"7" names trapping the dribbler from the weakside. To accomplish this, X1 must turn 1 as he crosses the half-court marker. X2 knows this and races hard toward 1, reaching 1 just as he reverses directions. X2 and X1 trap 1. X4 takes the habit pass (the strongside lane), and X4 shades the middle lane. X3 covers the middle lane, and X3 shades the weakside lane. X5 comes upcourt a step or two to offer help (Diagram 5-7).

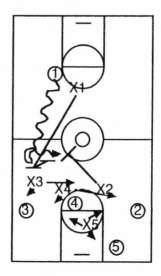

DIAGRAM 5-7

Should 1 pass successfully to 2, X4 would take 2, X3 would have 4, and X2 would pick up 3; X1 stays with 1, and X5 guards 5. A completed pass to 4 puts X3 on 4, X4 on 2, and X2 on 3. X1 and X5 keep their assignments. A completed pass to 5 or to 3 would have all defenders recovering onto their original assignments.

"27," like "26," is used to eliminate the great point guard as a threat. Should 1 continue dribbling, the trap stays in place. The interceptors adjust their positions. This means that for 1, the point guard, to be effective he must fight a double-team all night long. This is hard even for the great ones to do.

"27" and "26" can be coupled with the "8" calls to trap other weaker ballhandling guards, thereby creating turnovers. Suppose you know the 2 guard is a weak dribbler. You call "48" – "26," denying the point guard the ball. The pass comes into the 2 guard. You have "26" following the "48" call. As the 2 guard crosses the half-court line, he is trapped. This weak ballhandling guard may turn the ball over.

"28"

"8" names denying a designated attacker the ball and trapping once he gets it back. In Diagram 5-8, the point guard has

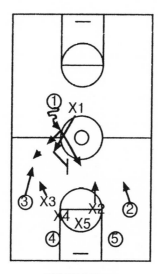

DIAGRAM 5-8

been named the designated attacker. It could just as well have been the shooting guard, etc. Once 1 passes to 3, X3 shades 3 so his body is between 3 and 1 but without allowing 3 to drive to the basket. X1 immediately jumps into the passing lane between 3 and 1. Should 1 free himself for a pass from 3 (or any other attacker), a player named by you goes to help trap 1. The player you name should be a non-shooting, non-penetrating perimeter player. If you must decide between penetrating or shooting, you must weigh which is more important to your opponent. A post defender could even be used to help trap 1 (see the next section). This is what makes the adjustable press so great.

There is no trap until 1 gets the ball back, so there is no need for either the coverage or the recovery rules. Should 1 get the ball back, you would then have to determine which defenders would rotate according to the rules. By now that should be easy.

"8" calls can be used to take any player out of his offensive game. All game long, the player to be taken out of his game encounters face-guard denial defense until he gets the ball; then he faces a double-team. This would limit the effectiveness of any offensive player.

"29"

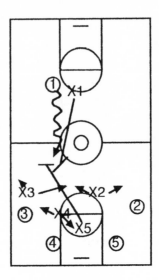

DIAGRAM 5-9

"9" names trapping with a designated trapper (can be combined with "8" calls). In the case of Diagram 5-9, the designated trapper is the post player (in the previous section, I discussed it using a wing player—so you have two options). As 1 dribbles cross the half-court line, X5, who has cheated up the court, races hard to help X1 trap 1. There is no middle-lane attacker, so X3 covers the strongside lane and shades the middle lane. X2 guards the middle lane and shades the weakside lane. X5 covers both 4 and 5 (Diagram 5-9).

A completed pass to any player sees the assigned defender covering his assignment, except in the case of a completed pass to 4 or 5. In those cases, X4 would cover the new receiver. The weakside wing would cover the other post player (for example, 1 passing to 5 would find X4 on 5 and X3 on 4). X5 would cover the open wing player. The other wing keeps his assignment, as does X1.

"9" calls coupled with "8" calls and the trap calls can eliminate any offensive player as a threat. To take a wing player out of his game, use "1," "5," "8," and "9." To take the point guard out of the attack, use "1," "6," "7," "8," and "9." The next chapter discusses how to eliminate the post players as threats.

The 20 series has been discussed from tactics "0" through "9." In each section, I have tried to show how the coverage and the recovery rules work. Also, I have discussed the best reasons for running that particular call. You may use the diagrams as drills if you decide that particular call will be in this week's game plans.

In the next chapter, I present the calls that will eliminate the post player as the attacker who will beat you. I also show how to attack the attackers by trapping their drives and their screens. Drives and screens can hurt any defense in the ten area or inside the ten. Trapping these drives and screens will reduce the effectiveness of these offensive maneuvers.

Chapter 6

How to Teach the 10 Series

The first five chapters presented the entire pressure defense, explained the fundamentals and basic elements, enunciated the tactics, and discussed the coverage and recovery rules—all in the hopes the ball would never reach the scoring area. But, alas, it will get there. So you must have a strong defense inside and around the ten area. That is the subject of this chapter.

"10"

"0" dictates the basic defense. "20" is always better than "10" because it compels the defense into a much more aggressive nature. But there is a time to run "10." When you do not respect the outside shooting of the opposition, "10" is a perfect call. It will frustrate the opponent. "10" also works well against teams that repeatedly try to force the ball inside to their big men.

"11"

"1" names a designated trap with a named ball movement. Many teams love to screen and roll, using a big player and a good ballhandling guard. The "11" call removes this offensive maneuver as a threat. In Diagram 6-1, the offensive post player, 5, comes

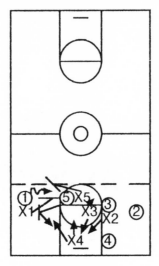

DIAGRAM 6-1

to the wing to screen for the point guard, 1. As 1 drives around the screen, X5 jumps into the dribbling lane. X1 races hard over the screen to help X5 trap 1. X4, who began to cheat when he saw the play developing, covers the rolling post player, 5. X3 covers the other passing lane, cheating in the direction where 1 looks. X2, per the coverage rules, plays safety, guarding 4 and the basket.

A completed pass to 5 finds X4 rotating onto 5, X2 keeping 4, X3 guarding 3, and X5 rolling back into the middle before picking up 2. X1 stays with 1. A completed pass to either 2, 3, or 4 impels all defenders to stay with their assignments.

Running "11" eliminates the screen and roll as an effective offensive maneuver. Good scouting reports will tell you when teams intend to use the screen and roll as an integral part of their offensive plans. "11" renders their practice sessions obsolete, frustrating the players who comprise their team.

"12"

I do not like to run and jump this close to the basket. It can be practiced if you so wish, and it can be used somewhat effectively. But great guards are taught to spin out of maneuvers, leaving this great guard the drive to the basket, and it is too close to the basket for the defense to recover. If you intend to run and jump near the basket, I would recommend following "12" with an immediate "17."

"13"

"13" names a three-man run and jump. Under no circumstance should "13" be called. There is not enough space to effectively run and jump with three men.

"14"

"14" calls a hedge and recover. This coupled with "10" eliminates most of the offensive inside game. When you are convinced you cannot be beaten with perimeter shooting, excessive use of the "14" calls will make the night very long for your opposition.

There are no traps, so, there is no need for the coverage or the recovery rules. All players guard their assignments.

Run "14" to complement "10," forcing the opponent to beat you with the outside shot. "14" eliminates the drive, and "10" reduces the pass inside. That leaves only rebounding the ball inside. Box out and get a hand in the shooter's face, and victory is yours.

"15"

Your opponent has a great shooting perimeter player. He is also good at penetrating and shooting. "15" is the perfect call. 1, the point guard, passes to 3, the great player (Diagram 6-2). X3 initially sags inside to help stop the penetration by 1 and also to show the passing lane open to 3. When 3 receives the pass, X3 races hard to keep 3 from driving the baseline. X1 comes to help X3 trap. X1 might want to sag off 1 as 1 dribbles, so X1 would be closer to 3 when 3 receives the pass. X4 covers 4 and shades the baseline, playing 3's eyes. X5 guards the middle lane and shades

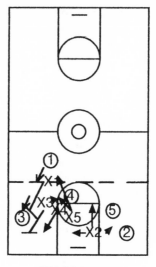

DIAGRAM 6-2

the passing lane back to 1, per the coverage rule. X2 plays safety, covering the basket area but also looking for an errant pass over to 5. The trap keeps 3 from shooting or driving. He must beat you with the pass, his weakest offensive maneuver. You have, with "15," taken this great player out of his game. Attackers can only shoot, penetrate, or pass. You have determined through scouting that 3 is a great shooter and a great penetrating attacker.

A completed pass to 4, 2, or 5 will have all defenders guarding their assignments. A pass to 1 would find X5 covering 1, X4 guarding 4, X2 keeping 2, X3 staying with 3, and X1 rotating to pick up 5, per the recovery rules.

"15" is perfect for eliminating the effectiveness of a perimeter player who is a great shooter or a great driving-shooting type of player. It will compel this great player to beat you with a pass, his weakest offensive maneuver.

"16"

"6" names trapping the dribbler from straight on, making this call perfect to use against teams that love to drive the

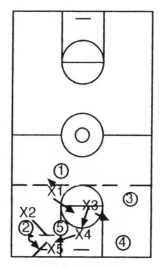

DIAGRAM 6-3

baseline. As 2 dribbles on a baseline drive, X5 comes off 5 and places his left foot on the out-of-bounds line, requiring 2 to stop his drive and pick up the dribble. X2 has guarded 2 on his drive by refusing to let 2 cut back toward the middle of the court (Diagram 6-3). This makes an ideal trapping area. The baseline acts as a third defender, and the open area is a pass back to the area just vacated by 2 (there is no attacker there). X4 must be alert to this maneuver, but that is why you practice. X4 covers the habit pass, the pass to 5. X1 can sink to help on the pass to 5, and X1 can shade the pass back to 1. X3 drops to cover the weakside basket area, playing safety as mandated by the coverage rules.

A completed pass to either 1 or 3 would see all defenders again picking up their assignments. A completed pass to 5 compels X4 to cover 5, X3 to guard 4, X1 to pick up 1, X2 to stay with 2 (maybe even doubling down on 5), and X5 to race to 3. A completed pass to 4 compels the same recovery as outlined above.

Through scouting you know your next opponent has two or three perimeter players who love to drive, especially the baseline. "16" would be your tactic. After several traps along the baseline, most teams will give up on this offensive maneuver, discarding this basic weapon.

"17"

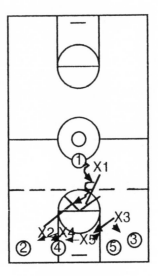

DIAGRAM 6-4

All of us will, some time in our career, face the great point guard. Diagram 6-4 displays a popular set used by teams with great point guards. "7" names trapping the dribbler from the weakside. As 1 begins his dribble-penetrating move, X2, who has cheated toward 1, races to trap. X4 covers the habit pass to 2 and shades the pass inside to 4. X5 rotates toward 4, but also shades 5. X3 has become the safety, guarding the pass inside to 5, as demanded by the coverage rules.

A completed pass to either 3, 4, or 5 compels the defenders to guard their assignments. A pass to 2 sees X4 take 2, X5 cover 4, and X3 guard 5. X1 keeps 1, possibly running the "8" maneuver, denying 1 the ball back; and X2 would rotate over to cover 3.

"17" is excellent for stopping the great dribbling point guard; when it is coupled with "18" (denying the pass to a designated player, then trapping that player), the great point guard cannot beat you with the maneuvers he does best. As always, when you are making a decision about which defensive tactic to use, you must take into consideration the talents of all players on the opposing team as well as the skills of your own players.

"18"

"18" names denying a designated player the ball and trapping once he gets it. The previous section showed this occurring against the great point guard; the next section reveals this transpiring against the great post player.

"18" should be paired with another defensive tactic. In the case of the point guard, "17" and "18" make a lovely couple. In the case of the post, "18" and "19" make a beautiful blend.

"19"

DIAGRAM 6-5

"9" names trapping with a designated trapper by pass or dribble. "19" would, therefore, allow us to trap any pass into a post player. Diagram 6-5 shows a double-down tactic as the post player receives a pass.

Diagram 6-5 shows 1 passing to 3. This occurs because you do not want the pass coming into the post from outside; so X5 plays the high side of 5 as long as the ball is above the free-throw line extended. Once the pass goes below the free-throw line, as in Diagram 6-5, the pass goes to 3 and X5 moves behind 5, opening up the passing lane inside to 5. But as this perimeter pass occurs, X1 and X2 cheat toward 5. X3 covers 3 tightly, unless 3 is not an offensive threat. When 3 passes inside to 5, X2, the weakside guard, doubles down on 5, erasing 5's immediate move to the basket. X5 covers the baseline side of 5 as the pass is entered. X2 defends any move by 5 to the inside. X2 and X5 both get against 5, even legally bumping him if necessary. 5 has never had inside rebounding position, and now 5 cannot make a move. 5's only recourse is to pass the ball to a perimeter player.

X1 checks both 1 and 2 while 5 has the ball (Diagram 6-5). A pass from 5 to 3 finds all defenders guarding their own assignment. A pass to 4 puts X4 on 4, X1 on 2, X2 on 1, X5 on 5, and X3 on 3. A pass to either 1 or 2 reveals X1 taking the receiver and X2 taking the other attacker. All other defenders stay on their assignments.

Of course, you could program 1 or 2 to cut to the basket when a double-down occurs. You can defense this offensive maneuver by letting the weakside defender, X4, step in to intercept the pass; or you can allow X1 to guard the cutter. In the latter case, the other perimeter player would be open for a three-point shot. You must know your personnel and the intentions of the opposition.

Instead of doubling down with a perimeter defender, you can double-down with a post player. This puts your two tallest defenders on the ball, forcing a higher lob pass out of the trap; your three quickest players gamble for interceptions. There is not enough space here to cover every possible type of double-down. You must know the strengths of your personnel and determine how you intend to make use of the double-down trap.

"19" is best coupled with "18" to stop the great post player. As you can see by Diagram 6-5, 5 never has rebounding position on any shot from the perimeter; 5 never has a drive or a shot unless he is attacking two defenders. 5 only has the open passing lanes to either 1 or 2. You have taken the ball out of 5's hands. He cannot beat you. You are impelling the other four attackers to beat you.

In this chapter you have seen traps set when the major part of your opponent's offense is the screen and roll ("11"); you have met the baseline drives with a trap ("16"); by use of the trap you have reduced the effectiveness of the great point guard ("17"), of the great post player ("19"), of the great shooter who penetrates ("15"); and you have kept these great players from getting the ball ("18"). You have coupled two tactics together to impel the other, weaker attacker to beat you. If your team members are too slow to run the 20, 30, or 40 series, the 10-and-inside-the-10 series is enough to completely disrupt your opponent's offensive plans. There is a defensive system for any type of personnel; it is your duty to decide what is best for your team for any particular year.

You have a complete defensive system that is aggressive and capable—capable not only of disrupting the offensive team's plans, but also of forcing turnovers. You can adjust your defensive system by expanding or contracting it at your will, as your personnel dictates. You can further adjust it by changing tactics. You can eliminate the favorite options of your opponent. You can compel the ball to an area, then trap it; or you can force the ball to a particular attacker, then trap him; or you can completely confuse the team attack by switching tactics strategically. And the entire defensive system is taught out of man to man. Because it develops from only ten tactics that can be used at any court marker, you really don't confuse your defenders by having to teach too much. But the offense must learn all kinds of different maneuvers if they are to successfully attack your defense.

In the next chapter I show you how to follow one tactic with another successfully. I illustrate the trap series only and parade a series of traps in the same possession by showing how you can trap a second pass down the sideline. I also display how to prepare your game plan and how to adjust that game plan from the bench during the game.

Chapter 7

How to Teach and Plan Combinations

In this chapter you will learn how to set a second trap during any possession. You will see how this is accomplished by making two calls (one tactic followed by another), or by teaching the second trap as an integral part of the defense. Or you can teach the entire defense, using only traps. One section is devoted to preparing a game plan; another section shows you how to adjust your defense during the course of the ball game.

The adjustable area man-to-man press has so far developed only one trap per possession. The next five sections show you how to develop a second trap during any possession. You should teach the second trap if your players are experienced enough with your defense or if you want an extra-aggressive nature to your defense. The defense has carryover value: After the first year, the second trap should definitely be taught. Opponents will never be able to teach enough press offense to defeat your press.

TRAP A SECOND PASS DOWN THE SIDELINES

You can always teach a second trap down the sidelines, which is the subject of this section. From this, and the next four sections, you can formulate a second trap from whatever maneuver suits your personnel.

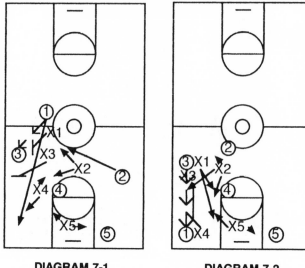

DIAGRAM 7-1   **DIAGRAM 7-2**

Diagram 7-1 displays the "25" tactic. The offensive maneuver is a variation of the old UCLA power game. 1 passes to 3 as 1 crosses the midcourt line (Diagram 7-1). X3, who had sagged originally, encouraging the pass to 3, goes over to trap 3. X1 races hard to help X3 trap. X2, who cheated toward the middle of the court because he knew the "25" tactic was called, covers the middle lane and shades the pass back to the midcourt area per the coverage rules. X4 defends the downcourt lane and shades the middle lane per the coverage rules. X5 plays safety and keeps 5 from getting the pass.

1, after passing to 3, cuts through the defense, running the UCLA power game. 3 successfully passes out of the trap to 1 in the corner (Diagram 7-2). Now you must have a new set of coverage rules if you are to trap a second pass down the sideline (these are really teaching points):

1. The player designated by the coverage rules contains the new attacker while waiting for his teammate to help trap.

2. The original trapper on the side of the downcourt pass becomes the second trapper.

3. The other original trapper races to cover the deep middle lane and shades the nearest middle lane.

4. The original upper-lane-coverage player now covers the middle lane and shades the pass back to the upper lane.

5. The original safety still plays safety but can help on any errant middle-lane pass.

By activating these rules, X3 would help X4 trap 1. This is a natural defensive movement, making it easy to teach. X1 would guard the new middle lane, the low post area, while shading the old middle lane, the pass to 4. X2 would defend the new middle lane, the pass to 4, while shading the new upper lane, the pass to 3, or the old upper lane, the pass to 2.

I have found it best to teach the second trap at the half-court level before extending it down the floor. The defenders usually see the coverage lanes and recovery rules easier at the half-court level.

From Diagram 7-2, the recoveries would be as follows: A successful pass out to 2 would find all defenders recovering onto their assignments. A successful pass out to 3 results in X2 covering 3, X1 guarding 4, X4 defending 1, and X3 taking 2. X5 would keep 5. A successful pass to 4 keeps X1 on 4, X3 on 3, X2 on 2, X5 on 5, and X4 on 1.

RUN AND JUMPS FOLLOWED
BY TRAP OF A PASS

I open almost every game with "40" into "20" because this tells me immediately how the opponents intends to break our press. Run and jumps followed by a trap usually thoroughly bewilder the opponent's offense. I show this combination by going from "42" into "25," to show run and jumps into trapping a pass, the subject of this section; I show the combination of run and jump into trapping a dribble, using "43" into "36" in the next section.

Diagram 7-3 exhibits the two-man run and jump (the "42" part). X1 guides 1 down the left sideline. X3 races hard toward 1, keeping his body between 1 and 3. All other defenders sag toward the middle of the court to offer help. When X3 gets near 1, he comes under control, intending to compel 1 to dribble to the right side of the court. But this really does not matter because the "25" part can be run to either side. But it requires more time for 1 to dribble to the right side, giving the defense more time to adjust.

Diagram 7-4 follows from Diagram 7-3 and displays the "25" part of the "42" – "25" call. As 1 crosses the midcourt line,

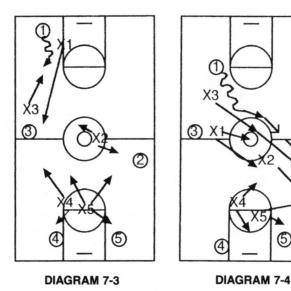

DIAGRAM 7-3   **DIAGRAM 7-4**

he will see X2 sagging, preventing 1 from continuing downcourt with his dribble. This sag by X2 opens the passing lane to 2. 1 can easily see this. 1 passes to 2, activating the "25" call. X2 prohibits 2 from driving downcourt after he has received the pass. X3 races hard to help X2 trap 2. X1 covers the middle lane and shades the pass back to 1, per the coverage rules. X5 denies the pass downcourt and shades the middle lane, per the coverage rules. X4 plays safety and offers help on any slow errant pass.

Should 2 pass to either 3, 4 or 5, X2 would guard 2, X5 would cover 5, X4 would defend 4, and X1 would watch 3. X3 would pick up 1. Should 2 pass back to 1, all defenders would guard their original assignments.

This example should allow you to plan two-man run and jumps followed by a trap of a pass. You would want to consider this combination when the opponent's point guard is a very good dribbler and the wings are poor passers.

RUN AND JUMPS FOLLOWED BY TRAP OF A DRIBBLER

I use a "43" tactic (three-man run and jump) followed by a "36" call (trapping a dribbler from straight on) to illustrate this combination. The last section dealt with a forty call into a twenty

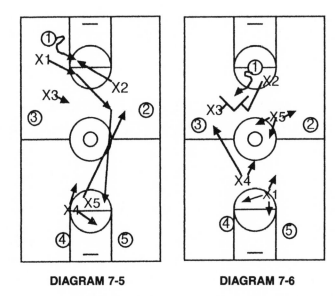

DIAGRAM 7-5   **DIAGRAM 7-6**

call; this section specifies a forty call into a thirty call. From this you can easily see how one can create combinations at will to harass any offense.

Diagram 7-5 shows X2 beginning the three-man run and jump as 1 begins his dribble toward 2. X2 keeps his body between 2 and 1, forcing a lob pass that might be intercepted by X5, who cheated forward as 1 received the inbounds pass. If the two-man run and jump has been used earlier, 1 just might throw his lob pass for the easy interception. X1 rotates all the way back to 5 to complete the three-man run and jump. X4 and X3 shaded toward the middle lane to offer help and to intercept any slow errant pass.

Diagram 7-6 is a combination from Diagram 7-5. X2 compels 1 to dribble down the left sideline. X3 races to trap 1 as 1 comes across the thirty marker. X2 stays to help trap. X4, per the coverage rules, guards the habit pass (the sideline attacking lane) and shades the middle lane. X1, who had earlier run and jumped, is the safety, per the coverage rules, defending any long pass to either 4 or 5. X5 defends the middle lane while shading the pass crosscourt to 2.

A completed pass to 3 finds X4 on 3, X1 on 4, X5 on 5, and X3 dropping to cover 2. X2 stays with 1. A completed pass to 2, 4, or 5 would send X3 back to 3, X5 onto 2, X4 with 4, and X1 onto 5, per the recovery rules.

A three-man run and jump combined with a trap of the

dribble plays havoc with the mind of any point guard. It will also impel many turnovers if the point guard is small in size, regardless of his quickness.

RUN A TACTIC FOLLOWED BY TRAPPING A DESIGNATED BALLHANDLER

From your scouting you know your next opponent always wants the point guard to set up their offense. You also noticed their center throws the ball inbounds, then trails their press offense as a safety value, and you know their center cannot penetrate with a dribble. That is the way they attack the press. So you decide to take the point guard out of the game by using the center's defender as the double-team trapper. You run "45" – "28" to accomplish this conscious defensive decision.

Diagram 7-7 shows "45." Keep in mind that all defenders are denying their assignments the basketball. If 1 cannot get the basketball, then a weaker attacker must bring the ball upcourt, and you are still going to prevent 1 from getting the ball back. You could alter this by calling "48" – "28." Both plans should be part of your game plan. (See "How to Prepare Your Game Plan"

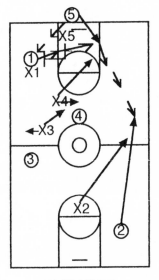

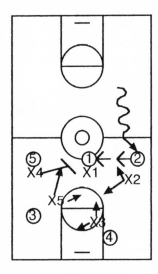

DIAGRAM 7-7   **DIAGRAM 7-8**

later in this chapter.) In Diagram 7-7, 1 receives the pass from 5. X5 races to help X1 trap 1. X4 guards the habit passing lane back to 5 and the middle lane to 4, per the coverage rules. X3 guards the downcourt passing lane and shades the middle lane. Actually more defensive pressure should be applied to 4 and 3 because you know 5 will not dribble with the basketball. Diagram 7-7 displays 2 breaking to half-court to receive the pass from 5 after 1 passes to 5. But 2 has been trained to wait and let 1 set up the offense. Once 1 passes to 5, X1 gets into denial position against 1.

Diagram 7-8 exhibits 2 trying to get the ball back to 1. 1 manages to free himself with a V-cut. Immediately X4, who is now guarding 5, activates "28" by coming to help X1 trap 1.

A successful pass back to 2 would not begin the offense, but X2 would guard 2, X4 would go back to 5, X1 would again deny 1 the ball, X5 would keep 3, and X3 would defend 4. These are the attackers picked up by the defenders when 1 successfully passed to 5 in Diagram 7-7. A successful pass to 5 would find X5 on 5, X2 on 2, X4 on 3, X3 on 4, and X1 again denying 1 the ball. Now X5 would be the new trapper should 1 receive the ball again. A successful pass to 3 has X5 on 3, X4 on 5, X2 on 2, X3 on 3, and X1 again denying 1 the ball. X4, who would be guarding 5, would be the new trapper should 1 again free himself. A successful pass to 4 would result in X5 on 3, X4 on 5, X2 on 2, X3 on 4, and X1 again denying the pass to 1.

You can see how it would be most difficult for 1 to set up the offense each possession. You have successfully eliminated their practice preparation for your game. You now stand a better chance of winning. That is the major purpose of this press. Yet you did not have to teach anything new. You are doing what you did since you began teaching the adjustable area man-to-man press.

TRAP THE MIDDLE PASS
AS A SECOND TRAP

From the last four sections, you should be able to devise and drill on setting a second trap during each possession. Teaching your team how to trap the middle pass is another tactic that would guarantee you a second trap when the ball is entered into the middle lane. But the middle lane is the hardest to trap

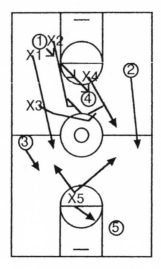

DIAGRAM 7-9

successfully because of the eight passing lanes out of it. I prefer to deny the pass into the middle lane and trap along the sidelines. But there is merit to teaching traps in the middle lane. It keeps constant double-team pressure on the basketball. That reason alone gives credence to teaching this trap. Also, if the middle-lane attacker dribbles downcourt, you can activate the flick from behind the dribbler (see Chapter 2).

Diagram 7-9 exhibits an often-used offense: It has a middle attacker who intends to receive the pass and dish the ball to the opposite outside lane (primary) or to the near-side lane (secondary). It has three outlet passes against the initial trap. You will see this type of formation often during your coaching career.

2 threw the ball inbounds to 1. "45" was your initial call. X2 races to help X1 trap 1. 1 immediately passes to 4. In Diagram 7-9, X4 would have initially covered the middle lane and shaded the pass back to 2. X3 would have defended the right lane and shaded the middle lane. X5, per the coverage rules, plays safety.

X3 must stop the immediate advancement of the ball by 4. X1, the trapper nearest the sideline, races hard to prevent the pass from 4 to the near-side lane. X4 does the same for the outlet to the far-side lane. If 2 leaves early to race up the sideline, X4 would drop as 2 leaves because X4 would not want to guard space. X5 knows this. X5 knows X4 can easily cover the cutting 2. So X5 shades more toward 3. A soft pass to 3 would permit X5 to must not watch the pass to 4. X1 must drop quickly to cover 3. X1 moves as the pass is on its way to 4. X2 comes to help X3 trap. Should 4 decide to dribble, X3 and X2 are on both sides of the ball, and they commence the stealing-from-behind maneuver discussed in Chapter 2.

TEACH THE BASICS
AND ONLY THE TRAPS

Probably the best press you can teach the first year is the basic defense, the "0," and the three primary traps, "5," "6," and "7." Teaching this from all the areas gives you exceptional double-team pressure for steals and a flawless basic team defense. This ammunition is all you need to win your ball games. It gives you enough in your defensive arsenal to take the team out of its team attack.

As the season progresses, you can add the "1," the "8," and the "9" tactics. Now your defensive scheme will include maneuvers that will take the point guard, the great perimeter player, and the terrific post man out of their offensive attack. You can now eliminate any offensive ploy that is a major part of your opponent's strategy. You can virtually dictate what your opponents will be allowed to do. You can stop their team attack, you can reduce the effectiveness of any player, and you can confuse and compel turnovers. You have an aggressive, yet safe, defense, all of which is taught from man to man, imposing individual duties and responsibilities, making it easy to correct any inferior decisions and performances. And you can adjust it at your whim. Now all you need to know is how to prepare that game plan and how to adjust it during the ball game. That is the subject of the next two sections.

HOW TO PREPARE
YOUR GAME PLAN

The preparation of the game plan begins in preseason: You want to decide how many tactics you are gong to teach. You want to drill the fundamentals, the tactics, the basics in your preseason practice sessions. This allows you later to merely "warm up" what you have already taught as the need arises.

Your second step is to get to know your personnel. Which of your defenders are the best trappers? Which of the taller players are your quickest? Which of the smallest are the best interceptors? These are the types of questions you must ask about your personnel.

After completely understanding your personnel, you want to scout your opponent (or better, get a film). From these reports you want to gleam how your opponent attacks a press. You want to know this from the forty, thirty, and twenty areas. You want to attack the spot where the opponent does not have three outlet passes designed in their press offense.

You want to determine which of your opponent's players cannot dribble-attack the basket, which cannot pass the ball well under pressure, which cannot beat you if you allow them to roam freely, and which players you must take out of the game if you are to win.

Based on the decisions you made in the above two paragraphs, begin to formulate a game plan. You do not want to overload your game plan. A few tactics run exceptionally well would be better than many tactics executed poorly.

An example: Let's say you know you must stop their big man. That means you will be using "18" and "19." Let's say you know their 2 guard is a good shooter but handles the ball rather carelessly. You infer from that the use of the "5" tactics because this impels the point guard to pass to the wing, and you intend to trap the wing. So you begin your plan with "45," "35," "25," and back into "18" and "19." Let's say you have determined their 4 player is a rebounder only. So you intend to use X4 as your trapper in the "18" and "19" tactics. Also, you might as well use X4 to help trap the 2 guard downcourt. So you now include denying the point guard the ball and trapping the 2 guard when he receives it, and you therefore add "49" and "39" to your game plan. Now you must practice this plan, but you also want to allow for a deduction mistake. So you also drill on having X2 act as the trapper in "18" and "19." You also want to further confuse the attack with another maneuver so you add "36" and "26" just as a diversionary tactic. Now you are ready to practice.

There is no way in any book to supply you with all possible game plans. You must read and reread this book until you are comfortable with making these very tough but often rewarding decisions. But even when you think you are really good at it, you'll find you make discretionary mistakes. So you must make adjustments during the game from the bench. That's the subject of the next section.

HOW TO ADJUST FROM THE BENCH DURING THE GAME

Your adjustments can be as simple as a substitute; you need a quicker interceptor or a taller trapper, for example. You know your personnel so you make the change.

Or your adjustment might require a change of a series or a tactic. You thought they had only two outlets at the thirty level; but, during the game, you found they actually had three, and they were hurting you. You go to the 20 series. They have to have a new offense, and your defense begins to force turnovers. Or you thought the 2 guard could not pass the ball well. You had been running "35." You adjust to "36" and find it's the point guard who is turning the ball over.

Your adjustments can involve rethinking while the game is in progress. Take the example from the previous section. You thought their 4 man would not hurt you so you used X4 to trap in "48," "49," "39," and "38," as well as in "18" and "19." But the opponent's players are throwing the ball long to their 4 man, breaking your press. And once they set up their half-court offense, their 4 man is killing you on the offensive boards while X4 rotates over to trap 5, using "18" and "19." You change to X2 as your trapper in "48," and "49." Now their press offense must find the new "open" player. And when they do find 2, 2 does not penetrate with the dribble, allowing full recovery by your defenders. Also, you use X2 to trap in "18" and "19." When 5 finds 2, 2 is not shooting well. You have taken 5 out of the game, and 2 has taken himself out of the game. From such adjustments, the game is won.

Your first rule of bench adjustment: DON'T BE AFRAID TO MAKE AN ADJUSTMENT. Too many good coaches don't want to cost their team a win; so often they don't HELP their team win. Fear of failure is your greatest obstacle.

Your second rule of bench adjustment: DON'T ADJUST TOO SOON. Frequently, your opponent will easily break your tactic in one possession. You should stay with the tactic a few more possessions unless you are convinced your opponent has solved that particular tactic.

CONCLUSION

A few years ago we were playing in the finals of the state tournament. We thought very highly of our opposition. They had been ranked number one in the state all year, and we had never been ranked. Out of too much respect, we stayed with "40" – "20" too long. They built a substantial early lead. We began to make adjustments. They began to turn the ball over and over and over. We got within one point and missed a three-pointer just seconds before the game ended. The newspaper the next day said they had finally figured out our press. They had not. Time just ran out before we could make one more adjustment for what would have been an unbelievable win. If there was a mistake, it was that we began to adjust too late.

The adjustable area man-to-man press will work best along the tournament trail. Unlike the basic zone and man-to-man presses, opponents cannot prepare for the adjustable area man-to-man press during their few practice sessions at tournament time. They will run the offenses they had prepared for seasonal play. They cannot adjust their press offenses at all four levels without completely confusing their team; neither can they adjust their personnel to do things they have not been doing all year long. But *you* can adjust. The adjustable area man-to-man press can be the great equalizer.